BODHISATTVA ATTITUDE

How to Dedicate Your Life to Others

What is better than bodhicitta in the life?
I am filled up with bliss. Even the hairs.

History
of immortals

HEART ADVICE is a series of core teachings—the "heart advice"— taken from the experiential instructions of Lama Zopa Rinpoche. The main resource is Rinpoche's major retreats, commentaries and transmissions since 2008, although other Archive materials supplement these. The goal is to preserve and make available Rinpoche's unique style and lineage of teachings and practices.

The HEART ADVICE SERIES is dedicated to the long life and perfect health of Lama Zopa Rinpoche, to his continuous teaching activity and to the fulfillment of all his holy wishes.

May whoever sees, touches, reads, remembers, or talks or thinks about this book never be reborn in unfortunate circumstances, receive only rebirths in situations conducive to the perfect practice of Dharma, meet only perfectly qualified spiritual guides, quickly develop bodhicitta and immediately attain enlightenment for the sake of all sentient beings.

Lama Zopa Rinpoche

Bodhisattva Attitude
How to Dedicate Your Life to Others

Edited by Sarah Thresher
Series editor Nicholas Ribush

LAMA YESHE WISDOM ARCHIVE • BOSTON
www.LamaYeshe.com

A non-profit charitable organization for the benefit of all
sentient beings and an affiliate of the Foundation for
the Preservation of the Mahayana Tradition
www.fpmt.org

First published 2012
6,000 copies for free distribution

LAMA YESHE WISDOM ARCHIVE
PO Box 636, Lincoln MA 01773, USA

Library of Congress Cataloging-in-Publication Data
Thubten Zopa, Rinpoche, 1945-
Heart advice : Bodhisattva attitude : how to dedicate your life to others /
Thubten Zopa, Rinpoche ; edited by Sarah Thresher.
pages cm. — (Heart advice series)
Includes bibliographical references.
Summary: "This book is drawn from Lama Zopa Rinpoche's essential teachings
given from 2008 onward. It is the first volume in LYWA's Heart Advice Series.
The topic of 'Bodhisattva Attitude' is how to develop bodhicitta by
practicing it throughout the day, from start to finish"—Provided by publisher.
ISBN 978-1-891868-27-6
1. Bodhicitta (Buddhism) 2. Buddhist meditations.
3. Spiritual life--Buddhism. I. Thresher, Sarah. II. Title.
BQ4398.5.T58 2012
294.3'444—dc23
2011053463

Cover photograph by Yew Kim Guan
Line drawing by Lama Zopa Rinpoche
Designed by Gopa&Ted2 Inc.

♻ Printed in the USA with environmental mindfulness on 30% PCW
recycled paper. The following resources have been saved: 20 trees,
620 lbs. of solid waste, 9,780 gallons of water, 2,168 lbs. of
greenhouse gases and 8.4 million BTUs of energy.

Please contact the LAMA YESHE WISDOM ARCHIVE for more
copies of this and our other free books

Contents

Publisher's Acknowledgments

We are extremely grateful to our friends and supporters who have made it possible for the LAMA YESHE WISDOM ARCHIVE to both exist and function: to Lama Yeshe and Lama Zopa Rinpoche, whose kindness is impossible to repay; to Peter and Nicole Kedge and Venerable Ailsa Cameron for their initial work on the ARCHIVE; to Venerable Roger Kunsang, Lama Zopa's tireless assistant, for his kindness and consideration; and to our sustaining supporters: Barry and Connie Hershey, Joan Thompson, Tony Steel, Vajrayana Institute, Claire Atkins, Thubten Yeshe, Roger and Claire Ash-Wheeler, Hawk Furman, Richard Gere, Doss McDavid, Therese Miller, Janet Hintermann, Nick and Gisela Dawson, Tom and Suzanne Castles, Doren and Mary Harper and other anonymous benefactors.

In particular, we thank the kind students of Amitabha Buddhist Centre, Singapore, for sponsoring the production of this book; Cecilia Tsong for organizing support for LYWA's new series, Lama Zopa Rinpoche's *Heart Advice*; and Diana Lim-Ng, Nicholas Weeks, Mimi Gay and Amitabha Buddhist Centre for major contributions to this project.

Special thanks are due to Venerable Sarah Thresher for not only suggesting the Heart Advice Series but also for editing the teachings that will go into the books in this series. Her excellent work on *Bodhisattva Attitude* indicates that these books will be of great benefit to many people and we thank her for it.

We are also deeply grateful to all those who have become members of the ARCHIVE over the past few years. Details of our membership program may be found at the back of this book, and if you are not a member, please do consider joining up. Furthermore, we would like to express our appreciation for the kindness and compassion of all those other generous benefactors who have contributed funds to our work. We value highly each and every donation and honor all our members and benefactors on our website.

Finally, I would like to thank the many other kind people who have asked that their donations be kept anonymous; my wife, Wendy Cook, for her support and editing skills; our dedicated office staff, Jennifer Barlow and Ven. Ani Tenzin Desal; our editors Ven. Ailsa Cameron, Ven. Connie Miller, Gordon McDougall and Sandy Smith; Ven. Kunsang for recording Lama Zopa Rinpoche; our transcribers Ven. Thubten Munsel, Ven. Thubten Labdron and Dr. Su Hung; Ven. Bob Alcorn for his work on our Lama Yeshe DVDs; David Zinn for his digital imaging expertise; our audio editors Jonathan Steyn and Mike Shaw; our e-publishing team Megan Evert and Sonal Shastri; Mandala Books and Wisdom Books for their help with our distribution in Australia and Europe and Amitabha Buddhist Centre and Losang Dragpa Centre for their help with our distribution in Singapore and Malaysia respectively; and everybody else who helps us in so many ways. Thank you all.

—*Dr. Nicholas Ribush*

Through the merit of having contributed to the spread of the Buddha's teachings for the sake of all sentient beings, may our benefactors and their families and friends have long and healthy lives, all happiness, and may all their Dharma wishes be instantly fulfilled.

Editor's Introduction

This book brings together several motivations taught by Lama Zopa Rinpoche to be used first thing each morning to generate a bodhicitta motivation and, on the basis of that, train the mind in the bodhisattva attitude.

The motivations were first taught during the opening days of a series of experiential lam-rim retreats called *Light of the Path*, highlighting at the very outset of the teachings the importance of motivation in our daily lives and activities. Several of the motivations were subsequently re-taught at various locations around the world and then collected together here.[1]

We can all understand the importance of motivation and attitude and how they affect the quality of our work and the result that can be achieved. Rinpoche particularly emphasizes the need for us to have a very clear direction and purpose in life. The real meaning of our lives is to bring both temporary and ultimate happiness to all sentient beings and to do this we need to achieve enlightenment. Enlightenment depends on first generating bodhicitta, and training our minds in these motivations and in the bodhisattva attitude helps us to do that.

In the introductory chapter of this book, *Everything Depends on Your Attitude*, Rinpoche explains why the mind plays such

---

1. See Technical Note below (p. 19) for a full list of teachings used in the book and how to access the original audio, video and transcripts at the LYWA website or FPMT Online Learning Center.

a crucial role in our lives and why having a good heart wishing to benefit all living beings is so essential. The following chapters contain two bodhicitta motivations that can be alternated each morning in our daily practice. The first and longest, *Cutting the Concept of Permanence* (chapter 3), is from sutra. The second and shorter, *Give Up Stretching the Legs* (chapter 4), is from tantra. A third motivation, *Four Wrong Concepts* (chapter 6), is specifically for taking the eight Mahayana precepts.

Each of these motivations is a guided lam-rim meditation aimed at directing our minds into at least an effortful thought of bodhicitta. On the basis of that, we can then train in the bodhisattva attitude (chapter 5). What is it, this bodhisattva attitude? It is the spirit of total and uncompromising dedication to the welfare of others—almost inconceivable in the vastness and courageousness of its prayer and aspiration to be and to do whatever is necessary to benefit every single living being. It is, of course, the attitude exemplified by Rinpoche himself. It is also the attitude Rinpoche seeks to cultivate in his students, centers and those around him.

The bodhisattva attitude is beautifully expressed in a selection of verses composed by the great bodhisattva Shantideva in *A Guide to the Bodhisattva's Way of Life*.[2] Rinpoche's advice is to recite and reflect upon these verses each morning after generating a bodhicitta motivation and then use them throughout the day as a guide and inspiration for how to think and behave differently.

In some ways, these *Bodhisattva Attitude* verses are reminiscent of the famous prayer attributed to St. Francis,[3] which directs our lives to selflessness and altruism. Similarly, this bodhisattva attitude opens our hearts to others and directs our minds towards enlightenment. Rinpoche explains that it is "totally against the

2. See chapter 1.
3. See appendix 5 for Rinpoche's adaptation of this prayer.

ego and totally opposite to the self-cherishing thought." There is only the wish to be *used* by others for their happiness.

The result of this way of practicing bodhicitta is deep happiness, peace, joy and satisfaction. How can this be so? Well, all of us seek happiness, yet we mostly fail to grasp the simple fact that happiness comes from cherishing others rather than perpetuating an ignorant and self-centered over-concern with ourselves. Rinpoche puts it quite simply:

> In the West, millions of people suffer from depression, but if you dedicate your life in the morning to numberless sentient beings, you will have unbelievable joy and happiness the whole day. Cherishing the I opens the door to all suffering, while cherishing others opens the door to all happiness. When you live your life every day for others, the door to depression, relationship problems and all such things is closed and instead there is incredible joy and excitement.
>
> With the bodhisattva attitude you become wish-fulfilling for others. All sentient beings have been wish-fulfilling and kind to you since beginningless rebirths and now you become wish-fulfilling for them. From this, all your wishes for happiness will be fulfilled, even your wish to achieve liberation and enlightenment and to benefit others by causing them to have happiness in this and future lives, liberation and enlightenment. You will become the cause of all this for others. This is how to overcome all problems.

Clearly, the bodhisattva attitude is a total and radical change from our habitual way of following the selfish mind and negative emotional thoughts and cultivating it requires determined and sustained effort. The goal of this book is to inspire and provide materials for anyone who wishes to do so.

THE IMPORTANCE OF GENERATING
A BODHICITTA MOTIVATION

Anyone who has ever met Lama Zopa Rinpoche will know that he embodies every quality of love and compassion. His joyful laughter, kindness and generosity are legendary; it is quite obvious that everything he does is for others. His own life is a powerful display of bodhicitta in action.[4] Not surprisingly then, in all of his teachings and practices Rinpoche emphasizes bodhicitta—from generating an extensive bodhicitta motivation at the beginning to making extensive bodhicitta dedications at the end.

Why is motivation so important? To understand this, we need to first be aware of how happiness and suffering come from our own minds. This is introduced in the opening talk, *Everything Depends on Your Attitude,* using a quotation from Lama Tsong-khapa's *Mind Training Poem*:

> White and black actions depend on good and bad
> thoughts:
> If you have good thoughts, even the paths and grounds
> are good;
> If you have bad thoughts, even the paths and grounds
> are bad.
> Everything depends on your attitude.

In Buddhism it is the mind and particularly the motivation that is the key factor in determining whether our actions become virtue and a cause of happiness or not. Rinpoche uses Kyabje Pabongka Rinpoche's example of four people reciting the *Twenty-One Praises to Tara* prayer to illustrate this:[5]

---

4. Ven. Roger Kunsang, Rinpoche's long time assistant, has described Rinpoche as "bodhicitta in a human form."
5. *Light of the Path*, 14 September 2009. Pabongka Rinpoche cites this in *Liberation in Our Hands, Part One*, p. 141.

The first person recites the Tara prayer with a motivation to achieve enlightenment for sentient beings and that person's prayer becomes the cause to achieve enlightenment and a cause of happiness for sentient beings.

The second person recites the prayer not to achieve enlightenment for sentient beings but only to achieve their own liberation from samsara, so that person's prayer does not become the cause to achieve enlightenment, but only to achieve liberation.

The third person recites the prayer not with a motivation to achieve enlightenment or liberation but just to achieve the happiness of future lives, samsaric happiness. That person's action does not become a cause to achieve enlightenment or liberation from samsara, but only for the happiness of future lives.

Up to now, all three people's action of reciting the Tara Praises has become Dharma. But the fourth recites the Tara prayer with a motivation only to achieve happiness for this life and this person's prayer does not become Dharma. It does not become holy Dharma but only worldly dharma. This is what we have to understand. That action is non-virtuous because the motivation is only for the happiness of this life and therefore the result will be only suffering.

There are four levels of happiness described here and in each case it is the motivation of the person reciting the prayer that determines which level is achieved. Normally, we might think that the action of reciting a prayer is enough to create virtue, but this is not so—it is our attitude that makes all the difference. Rinpoche comments on this story by warning us:

There is a similar story about two people who did Yamantaka retreat and one was reborn as a preta because his motivation was not Dharma.

There is a danger for this to happen to us. That is
why it is extremely important to examine the motivation at the beginning of any action, and if it is not
Dharma to make it Dharma. This is how to practice. When your motivation is Dharma, your actions
become Dharma and the result is happiness. Otherwise
you cheat your whole life because you believe you are
practicing Dharma but you are not.

Therefore, if we want happiness, we have to pay very close attention to our minds and our intention. The whole point of setting
a correct motivation from the very beginning of the day when
we wake up is to make sure that all of our actions from morning
to night do actually become virtue and a cause of happiness and
none are wasted.

The best motivation is bodhicitta. Why? Because bodhicitta is
the direct cause of enlightenment and the gateway to the Mahayana path. Training our minds in bodhicitta collects the inconceivable merit from which all other happiness comes and easily
purifies unimaginable negative karmas.[6] In *Cutting the Concept of
Permanence*, Rinpoche describes bodhicitta as the "very essence
of Dharma and the best way to make this life meaningful."

Therefore, if we let our actions be guided by bodhicitta they
will all become Dharma, and the happiness of this and future
lives will come by the way without even seeking it. On the other
hand, if our motivation is simply the happiness of this life, there
is no guarantee we will succeed. Of course, most people are
simply not aware that there is any happiness beyond this life
and therefore their whole lives are spent seeking only that. Since
they have no understanding of the correct cause of happiness, it
is hard to say if they will ever find it.[7]

6. For more on the benefits of bodhicitta, see *Liberation, Part Three*, pp. 99–120.
7. See *Light of the Path*, 13 September 2010. There are four levels of happiness—the
happiness of this life, future lives, liberation and enlightenment. The happiness of

Knowing how to practice Dharma

There are two types of motivation, the motivation before the action—the "motivation of the cause"—and the motivation while engaging in the action—the "motivation of the time." In a teaching given at Tushita Meditation Centre, Rinpoche recalls that the first question he ever asked Kyabje Chöden Rinpoche was, "For an action to become virtue, which is more important—the motivation of the time or the motivation of the cause?" To which Chöden Rinpoche replied, "The motivation of the cause."[8]

The example of the four people reciting Tara prayers shows us that it is the motivation for doing the action that determines whether it becomes virtue, not the action itself. Bodhisattvas, for example, can engage in actions that *appear* non-virtuous, yet they are transformed into virtue through the force of their pure bodhicitta motivation, just as a peacock can transform poisonous plants into nourishing food. Rinpoche often cites the story of the Bodhisattva Sea Captain,[9] a previous life of Guru Shakyamuni Buddha, who out of great compassion killed a trader who was planning to take the lives of five hundred merchants on board his ship. The captain could see with his immaculate clairvoyance the trader's evil intention and, unable to bear the suffering it would cause everyone involved, he took upon himself the negative karma and consequences of killing one person in order to save all the others. However, because his motivation was one of great compassion, the action became positive instead of negative.

If we can make both the motivation before the action and the

---

this life is not a goal in the path to enlightenment teachings and seeking it is not a Dharma action, but nonvirtue. However, it is explained that the happiness of this life comes naturally as a by-product of working for the other three levels of happiness. See *The Door to Satisfaction*, ch. 4.

8. Most Secret Hayagriva Retreat, 14 March 2010. Kyabje Chöden Rinpoche is an outstanding scholar, yogi and master of Sera Je Monastery and one of Rinpoche's gurus.

9. For example, in *Door to Satisfaction*, pp. 45–46.

motivation during the action bodhicitta by generating a bodhicitta motivation in the morning and maintaining it throughout
the day, all our actions will become a cause of enlightenment and
bring the greatest benefit and happiness to ourselves and others.
That means not only our "virtuous" actions of studying Dharma,
meditating, reciting mantras and so forth, but even what are
normally regarded as the "ordinary" actions of eating, walking,
sitting, sleeping and working. This is extremely important and
one definition of what is meant by "knowing how to practice
Dharma."[10]

One very powerful technique to keep our minds focused on
bodhicitta is to use a set of bodhicitta mindfulness practices
frequently taught by Rinpoche and included in the back of this
book.[11] At the end of each motivation we generate the strong
intention that all our actions become the cause of enlightenment and then use these mindfulness practices to keep that focus.
Throughout his teachings, Rinpoche explains many ways to integrate bodhicitta into every activity of our lives. We have to use
whatever method helps—our goal is not only to start the day
with bodhicitta but also to live our lives with bodhicitta all the
time. Rinpoche advises,[12]

> Even though you have generated a motivation of
> bodhicitta right at the very beginning of an action,
> still when you engage in that action it is very important
> to feel in your heart that you are doing it for sentient
> beings. For whom are you doing the action—for you

10. Rinpoche's definition of "knowing how to practice Dharma" is either knowing
all the different meditations involved with a practice such as *Lama Chöpa Jor Chö*
in order to purify and collect merit as extensively as possible, making the practice
most effective, or knowing how to make all our actions, spiritual and worldly,
virtuous. (*Sutra of Golden Light* Transmission, 20 March 2011).
11. See appendix 4. Rinpoche collected and translated these bodhicitta mindfulness
practices to be used in retreat and daily life.
12. 8 February 2010, Lama Serlingpa Bodhicitta Study Group, Jambi, Sumatra.

or for sentient beings? For sentient beings! The main concern should always be sentient beings. It is very, very good to try to feel this.

And,

> My general advice is to try as much as you can to live your life with a bodhicitta motivation whatever it is you are doing, whether you are working, studying Dharma, doing meditation or praying. Then you become a most unbelievably fortunate person. You are able to achieve enlightenment quickly, to be liberated from samsara quickly, and to quickly liberate and enlighten other sentient beings.

Even if we are unable to maintain a bodhicitta motivation throughout the day, if we have at least generated bodhicitta first thing in the morning, it will make a huge difference to our lives. When bodhicitta is our "motivation for life," as Rinpoche calls it, it transforms our actions into Dharma and the cause of enlightenment not only in this life but in future lives as well. Through the power of habituating ourselves to bodhicitta now, our future lives will again be drawn to bodhicitta and we will continue to practice in this way. If our present actions of eating, walking, sitting, sleeping, working and so forth are done with the thought to benefit all sentient beings, that will gradually bring us to the realization of bodhicitta, then up through the various pure and impure bodhisattva grounds to enlightenment. All these realizations start by training our minds in these bodhicitta motivations right now and then trying to live with bodhicitta all the time.

The most important thing is to make sure that our lives are not lived just to gain happiness and avoid suffering for one sentient being (oneself) but for *all* the numberless sentient beings. For many of us, this is a total and radical shift from habitual

self-centeredness to limitless altruism that may at first be difficult
to grasp. To give us a "picture" of what the mind of bodhicitta
would be like, Rinpoche gives this example: [13]

> There are numberless universes and in even one uni-
> verse, one country, one area, one mountain or forest,
> there are numberless ants, an unbelievable number
> of ants. Can you imagine living your life for them?
> Dedicating your life to serve them, to free them from
> suffering and bring them happiness? Not only tempo-
> rary happiness but also liberation from samsara and
> enlightenment. What could be better than that? There
> is no happier way to live life than with this bodhicitta
> attitude.

And, of course, when our motivation for life is bodhicitta, we are
cherishing not just numberless ants but *all* sentient beings and
living our lives only for them. Nobody is left out. In the *Bodhisattva Attitude*, Rinpoche says,

> The bodhisattvas' attitude is to always totally dedicate
> their lives day and night to be used by other sentient
> beings for their happiness. This is what they are seek-
> ing and wishing for all the time. You have to know
> that. If you feel like that, there is the opportunity to
> gradually become closer and closer to bodhicitta and
> have the realization. If you are able to change your
> mind into an attitude wishing to be used by others for
> their happiness, this is exactly what the bodhisattva
> attitude is.

13. 16 February 2010, Amitabha Buddhist Centre, Singapore.

Correcting mistakes in our practice

By understanding how everything depends on the mind, it becomes clear that we cannot judge whether an action is virtuous
or not by its appearance. Therefore, we need to be constantly
vigilant in our practice and not become complacent. Each of these
motivations guides us through key points of the lam-rim—which
Rinpoche calls "the *real* meditation"—and they are full of warn-
ings about what happens when Dharma is not practiced correctly.

In *Cutting the Concept of Permanence*, we are told that if we
live our lives with the concept of permanence, we will never be
able to give up attachment to the happiness of this life—which
is the very beginning of Dharma—and without that, none of our
actions will become holy Dharma, only worldly dharma. Our
lives will then be full of endless problems and expense:

> If the mind training in the meditation of imperma-
> nence is missing, look how much danger your life is
> in! There is no difference between a person who has
> met and studied Dharma and somebody who has not,
> between somebody who is a Buddhist and who is not,
> between somebody who has studied the philosophical
> or lam-rim teachings extensively and who has not. It
> is like that.
>
> You have to understand the point: sometimes there
> could be *even more* problems. Sometimes a person
> who has met Buddhism could have even more prob-
> lems than one who is not a Buddhist, because although
> there is greater education and more learning, the basic
> practice has not been done, and since the basic practice
> is missing, the problems could be even bigger.

In *Give Up Stretching the Legs*, we are told of the danger of not
putting effort into renunciation:

The world is full of examples showing how if you get attached to samsara and its pleasures thinking they are real happiness, you are totally cheated and suffer. In meditation, use as many of these examples as possible to get a clear understanding of the need to give up thinking samsara is good and engaging in it. This is very, very important. With this way of thinking, you can continuously practice Dharma. Otherwise, even if you try to practice, it doesn't really become Dharma, a cause to achieve liberation; it just becomes another cause of samsara because the motivation is attachment.

Throughout the teachings, Rinpoche warns what happens if we don't practice bodhicitta. For example, in the *Bodhisattva Attitude*:

I often hear people say, "Oh, these people are just using me!" Even sometimes at meetings in our centers I hear this. That is because they are not practicing bodhicitta. One time I wrote a letter to a center saying, "Bodhisattvas *want* to be used by sentient beings." That is what the bodhisattvas' attitude is. They actually accept it. The worldly mind thinks that being used by others is bad, the worst thing, but bodhisattvas are most happy to accept this.

In many ways, these motivations are not only to help us set up a bodhicitta motivation but also to examine, correct and heal any mistakes in our practice and lives that are causing problems. In *Cutting the Concept of Permanence*, Rinpoche says:

Like using a telescope to see something very far away or a microscope to see atoms or tiny sentient beings, similarly, here you use the Dharma to see your life and go beyond. By using Dharma wisdom you can see what is mistaken and what is correct; what is useless and what is useful; what is meaningless and what is meaningful; what is to be abandoned and what is to be practiced; what brings suffering and what brings happiness. It is all to do with the mind.

How to use this book

The Verses

The first section of this book contains the verses on the *Bodhisattva Attitude*. They were composed by the great bodhisattva Shantideva in *A Guide to the Bodhisattva's Way of Life*[14] and arranged into a prayer that appears at the end of the great lama Kachen Yeshe Gyaltsen's *chöd* practice. Rinpoche translates the verses from this prayer, so there is a variation in one of the lines.[15] Rinpoche also adds a concluding verse from the dedication chapter of Shantideva's *Guide*.

The verses are to be read each morning on the basis of one of the bodhicitta motivations to remind us how we are going to dedicate our lives to others. They can also be recited and contemplated throughout the day. The point is to try to remember and *live* in their meaning.

There are elaborate and abbreviated ways of reciting the *Bodhisattva Attitude*. The longer version consists of reciting all the verses; the shorter way is to recite just the last three or two verses, which cover everything. It all depends on time. There is a commentary to the verses in chapter 5 and a meditation combining the verses and Rinpoche's commentary in chapter 10.

14. See note 21.
15. See note 80.

The Teachings

The second section contains teachings on the motivations. In order to generate bodhicitta we need to train our minds in stages using a variety of methods and there is no better way to do this than by meditating on the lam-rim. With these motivations we train our minds in the whole path to enlightenment and particularly in the three principal aspects of the path—renunciation, bodhicitta and the wisdom realizing emptiness—which are the very heart of all the Buddha's teachings. Each of the motivations emphasizes a different aspect of these three principal aspects and each one has a different technique for bodhicitta, focusing mainly on the instructions for exchanging self for others.

Cutting the Concept of Permanence is the first and longest motivation. It begins with a meditation on impermanence and death and equalizing the eight worldly dharmas. Here the main emphasis is on counteracting our habitual ingrained belief that we are going to live for a long time, which is an obstacle to taking up serious Dharma practice. At the time of death our lives will appear to us like a flash of lightning that passed and finished so quickly, but up to that point ignorance blinds us with a false concept of permanence that makes us think we will live for a long time. If we do nothing to cut through this mistaken concept we will waste the precious opportunity we have to practice Dharma and secure the happiness of future lives up to enlightenment. How do we cut this concept? We need to understand that death can come at any time by training ourselves constantly in the thought that it can. On the basis of this, we then try to *feel* how precious this human life is and make the strong determination to engage in continual intensive Dharma practice—which means constantly integrating the three principal aspects of the path into our lives and living in vows.

In this motivation, having realized that we could die today, we decide that the most important practice for this and future lives is bodhicitta, and then train in the practice of exchanging self for others and taking and giving while reciting OM MANI PADME HUM.

The second motivation, *Give Up Stretching the Legs,* is shorter and based on a verse sung by the dakas and dakinis to awaken the tantric yogi from the sleep of clear light. Again, it begins with a reflection on impermanence and the need to give up attachment to this life and practice Dharma. However, the main emphasis in this motivation is on giving up attachment not just to this life but to all of samsara and its pleasures. This is extremely important because the stronger we can generate renunciation of our own suffering, the easier it will be when we turn our attention to others to generate aversion to their suffering as well and give rise to a strong bodhicitta intention.

We easily misunderstand what samsara is, thinking that it refers to all the pleasures of this life, which are real happiness. This makes it very difficult for us to want to achieve liberation. Therefore, Rinpoche begins by precisely defining samsara in a way that makes clear that it is only in the nature of suffering. There are three types of suffering—the suffering of pain, the suffering of change and pervasive compounding suffering. The suffering of pain is easy to understand—even animals can recognize this and want to be free from it. Most human beings, however, are totally unaware that their lives are afflicted by the other two sufferings and therefore have no thought of seeking liberation from them. Rinpoche focuses on the suffering of change, using a verse from the *Guru Puja*—"Samsara is extremely unbearable like a prison; please bless me to give up looking at it as a very beautiful, happy park"—to illustrate how our wrong belief that samsara and its pleasures are real happiness cheats us and keeps us continually circling in samsara, where every type of rebirth is pervaded by suffering.

In this motivation, we generate bodhicitta by contemplating a powerful Kadampa thought training advice:

I is the root of all negative karma; it is to be instantly
   thrown very far away.
Others are the originator of my enlightenment; they are
   to be immediately cherished.

"No matter what they do to you," Rinpoche says, "sentient
beings are always the originator of your enlightenment."

In the next chapter there is an explanation of the *Bodhisattva
Attitude* since these verses are to be recited following the previous two motivations. In all of these motivations, we are reminded
how kind and precious other sentient beings are; the stronger we
are able to feel this, the more natural it will be to cherish and
want to serve them—which is what the bodhisattva attitude is
all about. Our goal here is to generate the wish to totally sacrifice our lives for others—not just through prayer and reflection
but also through our attitude and actions; not just to one or
two people we like but to all; not just when we are in a good
mood but also when we are depressed; not just now but forever.
The stronger we are able to generate this bodhisattva attitude,
the deeper will be our own sense of well being and joy and the
quicker we will achieve enlightenment.[16]

The final motivation, *Four Wrong Concepts*, is for taking the
eight Mahayana precepts. It has a very succinct teaching on emptiness as well as a reflection on the specific sufferings of each of
the six realms that complement the previous motivations. The
four wrong concepts are the four mistaken ways of viewing the
world that have kept us trapped in samsara and suffering since

---

16. Rinpoche: "Whoever has stronger compassion for sentient beings and is able
to sacrifice their life from the heart to others can achieve enlightenment quickest."
This is illustrated by the story of Maitreya and Shakyamuni Buddha. Maitreya
generated bodhicitta first, but in a previous life, when they were both princes
and saw a starving tigress, although both had compassion, Buddha's compassion
was stronger and he was able to offer his body to the hungry tigress. Therefore
Shakyamuni Buddha became enlightened before Maitreya. (Lama Zopa Rinpoche
Australia Retreat, 14 April 2011).

beginningless time. The first two of these—viewing impermanent phenomena as permanent and suffering as happiness—have
already been dealt with in *Cutting the Concept of Permanence*
and *Give Up Stretching the Legs*. This chapter focuses on the
main wrong concept and originator of the others, which is ignorance—the self-grasping of the person and self-grasping of the
aggregates. In this motivation, Rinpoche guides us through a
short, powerful meditation on emptiness and explains how to
correctly identify the object to be refuted—the truly existent I.

This time when generating bodhicitta we reflect on sentient
beings' kindness in the following way:

> It is amazing how kind sentient beings are. They
> are kinder even than Buddha, Dharma and Sangha,
> because Buddha, Dharma and Sangha came from the
> kindness of sentient beings.
>
> By seeing that sentient beings are the most precious,
> kindest and dearest ones in our life, we are unbeliev-
> ably happy to do anything we can to help them.

As for the lineage of these motivations, Rinpoche received *Give
Up Stretching the Legs* from His Holiness Serkong Tsenshab Rin-
poche and *Four Wrong Concepts* from His Holiness the Dalai
Lama. *Cutting the Concept of Permanence* and the *Bodhisattva
Attitude* seem to originate from Rinpoche himself.

The introduction to the motivations, *Everything Depends on
Your Attitude*, sets up several major themes that run through
Rinpoche's teachings, such as the importance of the mind and
attitude, rejoicing, impermanence, bodhicitta, the urgent need
to meditate on the lam-rim and the importance of continual
purification and accumulation of merit.

At the very heart of the introduction is Rinpoche's story of his
early life studying philosophy at Buxa refugee camp and how he
met with the first ordained Westerners of the Tibetan tradition

at a young age. It is hard not to draw a comparison between the appalling conditions and hardships endured by the Tibetan monk exiles in the refugee camp at Buxa, who persevered with their studies and subsequently became great teachers able to spread the light of Dharma throughout the world, and the first Western nun who died tragically in a landslide in Darjeeling due to not heeding the call to immediately leave her cottage because she was busy packing money into a briefcase.

In *Four Wrong Concepts*, Rinpoche remarks:

> We have such unbelievable comfort and pleasure that we can't imagine it. We are totally spoiled and pampered—yet we are still unable to practice Dharma!

Rinpoche's own life-story calls upon us to reflect on the very root of the lam-rim teachings, the qualities and kindness of the spiritual master. These heart advice teachings are a wake up call to immediately put all that we have learned into practice.

The Motivations

The third section comprises the actual motivations. These contain the key-points extracted from Rinpoche's teachings. Each motivation is set up according to Rinpoche's advice and keeps closely to his words. Most have a long and a short version. Readers can use these to familiarize themselves with the key points and integrate them into their lives.

The Appendices

Finally, the appendices contain material to support the motivations and the bodhisattva attitude.

There is a set of *Morning Mantras* (appendix 3) to be recited before or after the motivations to increase the effect of all our actions and the benefit they bring others and ourselves. I have also included a concise version of Rinpoche's *Bodhicitta Mindfulness* instructions (appendix 4). This is a collection of slogans and yogas compiled by Rinpoche to help us maintain mindfulness on bodhicitta with each action that we do—walking, sitting, washing, sleeping, eating and so forth. The mindfulness practices are a very important tool for keeping our mind focused on the bodhisattva attitude. Both of the teachings in these two appendices were given at the same time as the bodhicitta motivations and the way of integrating these teachings is explained in *How to Start the Day with Bodhicitta* (appendix 1).

There is also a meditation on the stages of the path to enlightenment (appendix 2), Rinpoche's adaptation of the *Prayer of St. Francis* (appendix 5) and some useful reflections on the shortcomings of the self-cherishing thought, the advantages of cherishing others (appendix 6) and the great need for compassion (appendix 7).

TECHNICAL NOTE

Most of the transcribing in this book is my own, except in cases where the original audio recordings were missing. The main teachings used for each chapter are listed in the footnotes. The principal teachings referred to in this book are: *Light of the Path* Retreat, September 2009 (Archive number 1792) and 2010 (1838), Black Mountain, North Carolina, USA; Most Secret Hayagriva Retreat, March 2010, Tushita Meditation Centre, Dharamsala, India (1801); and two talks on motivation given at Shedrup Ling Center, October 2010, Ulaanbaatar, Mongolia (1844). Additional material and support was drawn from the 100 Million Mani Retreat, May 2009, Institut Vajra Yogini, Lavaur, France (1783); *Guru Puja* Commentary, February 2010, Jakarta, Indonesia (1796); *Lama Tsongkhapa Guru Yoga* Commentary, February 2010 (1795) and 2011 (1850),

Amitabha Buddhist Centre, Singapore; Refuge and the Twelve Links, June 2010, Hong Kong (1817 & 1820); Milarepa Retreat, September 2010, Milarepa Center, Vermont, USA (1840); *Sutra of Golden Light* Transmission, December/January 2010/2011, Kopan, Nepal (1855); *Three Principal Aspects of the Path*, February 2011, San Francisco, USA (1856); *Sutra of Golden Light* Transmission, March 2011, San Jose, USA (1859); Lama Zopa Rinpoche Australia Retreat, April 2011, Atisha Centre, Bendigo, Australia (1861).[17]

All translations are based on Rinpoche's own words and excerpted from the teachings unless otherwise indicated. In every case they are meant to convey the essence of Rinpoche's commentary rather than be a precise translation of the original Tibetan or Sanskrit. Throughout the text I have tried to preserve Rinpoche's voice. Rinpoche's comments on the translation of Tibetan terms have been put as footnotes.

Acknowledgments

This book began as a private project as I was inspired by the beauty of the *Bodhisattva Attitude*. In the first teachings I ever received from Rinpoche, he taught on this prayer to become like "the earth, water, fire and wind" for sentient beings.[18] That was many years ago, when I had never seen or heard of such a thing before, and since Rinpoche so clearly embodied the prayer, it deeply moved me.

Therefore, from beginning to end, I have nobody to thank but Rinpoche. I pray that the collective effort to publish this book may in some way repay his kindness in giving these teachings,

17. To access the original teachings, go to LamaYeshe.com and search for the Archive number (the number in brackets, above) using the "Search the Archive Database" link on the home page. Some of these teachings—such as *Light of the Path*—are also available in audio, video and transcript form along with related study modules at the FPMT Online Learning Center, onlinelearning.fpmt.org.
18. *Fifteenth Kopan Course*, November 1982 (Archive number 95).

act as a cause for his perfect health and long life and support his enlightened activity.

Many people were kind to and supportive of me as I worked on these teachings and I am extremely grateful to them all. Particularly I would like to thank Rowena Meyer in Santa Fe and Dr. Chiu Nan Lai, Ven. Chosang and family for helping me in Crestone. Thank you to Lynne Ingram and Nick Jablons; to Ale Almada, Jim and Cherie Sutorus; and to Amy Cayton and Annie Moon. Also Fabienne Pradelle, Heidi Oehler and everyone at Vajrapani and Denice Macy and everyone at Land of Medicine Buddha; both of these centers provided a place for me to work on the book, as did my dear friend Mary-Beth Harhen. Sarah Shifferd was always very generous with her editorial help and for technical assistance I relied on the patience, wisdom and kindness of Ven. Stephen Carlier, Ven. René Feusi, Ven. Tenzin Dekyong and Charles Smith. Ven. Jangchub, Ven. Yangchen, Ven. Jampa Michele and Miranda Reyna-Metzler also read the manuscript and gave valuable suggestions. Thank you to Ven. Kunsang for recording the teachings and Ven. Joan Nicell for typing the initial simultaneous transcripts.

The students at Amitabha Buddhist Centre, Singapore, sponsored the first booklet of *Bodhisattva Attitude*[19] for Chinese New Year 2011 and also funded this current book. I thank them all for their kindness, especially Tan Hup Cheng, Cecilia Tsong, Lim Cheng Cheng, Ng Swee Kim, Kennedy Koh and Shirley Ong, who took care of me during my visits to Singapore.

My deep thanks also to Dr. Nicholas Ribush, Wendy Cook, Jen Barlow and all at the Lama Yeshe Wisdom Archive. "Dr. Nick"—as we know him—along with Ven. Robina Courtin and Ven. Ailsa Cameron, has worked so hard for years to preserve, edit and publish Lama Yeshe and Lama Zopa Rinpoche's teachings. Thank you, Nick, for all your editorial work and patient

19. Copies of this may still be available from ABC and LYWA.

support as well as your encouragement and vision to create the Heart Advice Series.

Sarah Thresher
Lama Tsongkhapa Day
Crestone, Colorado
December 2011

Part 1. The Verses

---

*If you wish to benefit yourself, generate the sublime
thought of enlightenment,*

*If you wish to benefit others, generate the sublime
thought of enlightenment,*

*If you want to serve the teachings of the Buddha,
generate the thought of enlightenment,*

*If you desire happiness, generate the thought
of enlightenment.*

KHUNU LAMA RINPOCHE[20]

---

20. *The Jewel Lamp: A Praise of Bodhicitta*, v. 26. Translated by Lama Zopa Rinpoche, *Lama Tsongkhapa Guru Yoga* Commentary, 14 February 2010, Amitabha Buddhist Centre. (Khunu Lama Tenzin Gyaltsen's book has been published in English as *Vast as the Heavens, Deep as the Sea*.)

Nalanda Monastery, France

1. Bodhisattva Attitude[21]

The Verses

I shall give away fully with no sense of loss
My body, enjoyments and all merits of the three times (past,
    present and future)
To accomplish the work for all sentient beings.

By giving away all, I will be liberated from the oceans of
    samsaric suffering
And my mind will achieve the sorrowless state.
Since I have to leave everything (at death)
It is best to (now) give it away to every single sentient being.

Having given this body to sentient beings
To use *however* they want that makes them happy,
Whether they always kill, criticize, beat me or whatever,
It is totally up to them.

Even if they play with my body,
Ridicule me, put me down or make fun of me,

---

21. These verses are from the great bodhisattva Shantideva's *A Guide to the Bodhisattva's Way of Life*, ch. 3, vv. 11–21. Translated by Rinpoche from a prayer at
the end of Kachen Yeshe Gyaltsen's commentary to the *chöd* practice, which is in
volume 16 of his *Collected Works*. Rinpoche adds an additional concluding verse
from the *Guide*, ch. 10, v. 55.

Whatever they do, since I have given this body to them,
What is the point of retaliating?

Let this body only do actions that cause no harm to others,
And whoever looks at or thinks of me,
May it never be meaningless for them.

Whoever focuses on me—
Whether with anger or devotion—
May that always be the cause for them
To achieve every success.

May all who say unpleasant things,
Harm, mock or make fun of me
Have the fortune to achieve enlightenment.

May I become a guide for those who are guideless,
A leader for those who are entering the path,
A ship, a boat and a bridge
For all who wish to cross (over water).

May I become a beautiful garden for those who seek one,
A light for those who look for light,
Bedding for those who wish to rest
And a servant for all who want me as their servant.

Like a wish-granting jewel,
A wish-fulfilling vase, powerful mantra,
Great medicine and a wish-granting tree,
May I fulfill all the wishes of sentient beings.

Just like the sky and the great elements
Earth, (water, fire and wind),

May I always be the means of living and the cause
   of happiness
For sentient beings equaling the limitless sky.

As long as space exists,
As long as sentient beings exist,
May I too abide and eliminate the suffering of sentient beings.

Light of the Path

Part 2. The Teachings

Bodhicitta makes you abandon all harms,
Bodhicitta rids you of all sufferings,
Bodhicitta frees you from all fears,
Bodhicitta stops all negative conduct.
KHUNU LAMA RINPOCHE[22]

22. op. cit., v. 50.

Light of the Path

2. Everything Depends on Your Attitude[23]

An Introductory Talk

OUR LIVES HAVE BEEN MOST FORTUNATE

It seems that many old minds have come back, and however our lives have been up to now, that is extremely worthwhile.[24]

I would say that compared to others, our lives have been most fortunate. First of all, many of us have heard the heart of the Buddhadharma, the very essence of the 84,000 teachings of the Buddha, the very precious teaching on the stages of the path to enlightenment (*lam-rim*) many times. We have even heard this from His Holiness the Dalai Lama himself, who is the real living Chenrezig, the Compassion Buddha manifested in the human form of a monk—the aspect that can most perfectly guide us. Just that alone is most amazing and inexpressible. It is the most unbelievable, rare, fortunate and precious thing that could have happened to us this life.

Then we have met many other great teachers and unbelievably qualified virtuous friends who preserve the whole entire Buddhadharma—the Lesser Vehicle, Mahayana Paramitayana

23. This is the very first talk and introduction to *Light of the Path*, 9 September (afternoon) 2009. It has been edited along with additional material taken from *Light of the Path*, 20 September 2010, and Milarepa Retreat, 2 September 2010.
24. Here Rinpoche is addressing the older students who have come to attend the *Light of the Path* Retreat, some of whom attended their first meditation retreats with Rinpoche and Lama Yeshe in the early 1970s.

and Mahayana Tantrayana teachings. Particularly, many of us older students have met and received teachings and initiations from Lama Yeshe, who was kinder than all the numberless past, present and future buddhas and whose holy name is extremely rare and difficult to express.

So really, if we look at what has happened to us so far in this life, it is most amazing to have met many qualified virtuous friends who can reveal the complete path to enlightenment from their own experience. Can you imagine how most unbelievably fortunate our lives have been?

WE CAN'T REALLY TELL WHEN DEATH WILL COME

But of course, this incredible opportunity will not last long. It is just like lightning on a very dark night that for a short time reveals everything clearly and is then gone.

Life is not long and we can't really tell when death will come. There are many conditions for death, like the 400 different types of disease, 360 spirit possessions, 1080 interferers and these days there are new diseases that were never heard of before like swine flu. (There is no kangaroo flu yet—only pig flu!) Then there is cancer. We hear all the time about this and that friend or family member suddenly getting cancer. Up to now we have been hearing about our family members, friends, students and others having cancer, but how can you tell that sooner or later other people won't hear your own name with the word "cancer" next to it and a "has" in between? This happens to many people in the world. Already many older students we have known, who had been studying Dharma for some time, have passed away in different countries. We can never tell. We might be next. That is how life is.

Then there are many other sicknesses. For example, I have diabetes and that brings many symptoms. Sometimes I have been a friend of diabetes and sometimes an enemy. We cannot always live our lives with the concept of permanence, thinking "I am going to live forever." Well, maybe not "forever"—unless you are on drugs or hallucinating! But anyway, life is very short, and there is not much time left.

Generally, life is very short in degenerate times and even things that are supposed to support life can become the conditions for death. For example, medicines can have side effects leading to death and many people die when their houses collapse or while eating food.

SISTER VAJRA, FREDA BEDI AND MY EARLY LIFE AT BUXA

The very first Western nun to receive the Tibetan Buddhist lineage of ordination was called Sister Vajra. She died when her house collapsed in a landslide in Darjeeling.

I came to know Sister Vajra through an old pen friend that Freda Bedi found for me. Freda Bedi was a heart disciple of His Holiness Karmapa's previous life. I heard she was recognized by His Holiness Karmapa as Dorje Palmo and they made a throne for her in Sikkim.[25] There are high thrones for the lamas and also one for her. I am sure she must have originally been Christian and then I think she went to Sri Lanka to study Theravada Buddhism. Her son and daughter attended the same university as Pandit Jawaharlal Nehru's son and daughter and they became friends. She was appointed by Pandit Nehru to take care of the Tibetan monks after they escaped from Tibet. That is how she got connected to Tibetan Buddhism and she liked it.

25. His Holiness Karmapa is the head of the Karma Kagyü school of Tibetan Buddhism. Traditionally the monastic seat of the Karmapas is Tsurphu in Tibet, but the Sixteenth Karmapa came into exile and was based at Rumtek in Sikkim. The present Karmapa, who is the seventeenth incarnation, currently lives in lower Dharamsala, India. The throne for Freda Bedi would be for her recognized reincarnation.

Life at Buxa Duar

Freda Bedi came to Buxa Duar, West Bengal, where I lived for eight years. That was the place where I had a little fortune to receive some philosophical teachings and do some study and debate on the extensive scriptures. When the monks escaped from Tibet, they arrived at a place called Missamari in Assam, which was extremely unbelievably hot, and were then moved to Buxa. Not all the monks went to Buxa after escaping from Tibet; most were sent to work making roads in different parts of India, such as Dalhousie, Ladakh and West Bengal. At that time India was busy constructing roads around its border to protect the country from China. There were only around 1,500 monks who wanted to continue their studies and were able to go to Buxa. They stayed there for about ten years and studied unbelievably hard. Most of the key teachers, the abbots and ex-abbots, who are currently educating the monks at Sera, Ganden and Drepung monasteries in South India did their main study at Buxa. There were also a few monks from the Sakya, Kagyü and Nyingma traditions at Buxa who became great teachers.

Buxa had been a concentration camp during the British times. Pandit Nehru and Mahatma Gandhi-ji were imprisoned there. The very old building where Mahatma Gandhi-ji was imprisoned was surrounded by barbed wire three or four stories high. Some nuns from Tibet came and lived there, and it became a nunnery. Next to that was a long building. Some of the monks from Ganden Monastery lived in half of it and in the other half were monks from Sera Me and Sera Je. That was not the only place the monks lived, but as many of them as could fit lived there. It was a very tall building with one or two main entrances and barbed wire outside the front and back. When you entered inside, the narrow space was all lined with monks' beds. That same building where the monks lived was also the place where Sera Je and Sera Me would gather together to do puja. The older monks would sit on the beds, the other monks sat on the floor and the abbots sat up front with the incarnate lamas next to them.

Outside there was a courtyard and again it was lined with beds. On one side of the courtyard was the building wall and on the other side was barbed wire. In that courtyard there was a high bed for Geshe Rabten Rinpoche, who taught me the very first basic subject of debate. When I first met Geshe Rabten I was wearing a very long robe. It was a very tall, elderly monk's *shemthab* made of good quality wool, folded and wrapped around me, which made me look fat. I came with another person who brought a thermos of tea as an offering; I think there was no bread or anything else, just the tea. Geshe Rabten was sitting up on the high bed and I had to make my way between the beds all the way from the door. Down below Geshe Rabten sat Lama Yeshe with another monk. He had a huge pile of texts in front of him and was looking up at Geshe Rabten Rinpoche with great devotion. When I got there, Lama Yeshe picked me up and put me on Geshe Rabten Rinpoche's bed because I carry the name "incarnate lama."[26] Geshe Rabten taught me *Collected Topics,* which is like the A-B-C-D of debating, and after receiving that, I began my studies

Buxa was a very mischievous place. Many people had been killed there when it was a concentration camp and at first it was full of spirits. Some of the monks even went crazy. Later it became more and more peaceful. It was also unbelievably hot, with a very unhealthy kind of heat. Unfortunately, the monks didn't immediately try to copy the Indian lifestyle and way of eating food. If they had done so, more would have stayed healthy and survived. Of course, there were a lot of announcements and there was advice in the newspapers and from the Tibet Office in

26. Tib: *tulku.* Lama Zopa Rinpoche was recognized at a very young age as the incarnation of a great Nyingma tantric practitioner from Solu Khumbu called the "Lawudo Lama"; incarnate lamas are generally seated higher than ordinary monks. For more details on Rinpoche's previous and early life, see *The Lawudo Lama.*

Dharamsala, but many of the monks continued to eat the same way they were used to in Tibet, where it is very cold. There was a group of Tehor Khampa monks living next to us, who were used to eating uncooked meat in Tibet. In Buxa, it was so unbelievably hot that when they ate uncooked meat they had diarrhea for three months. Many monks got sick with TB or died because of the heat and the unhealthy living conditions. In one of the rooms where I stayed I could see through the door from my bed, and every week I would watch groups of monks pass by carrying the dead body of a monk from their house (*khang-tsen*) on their way to the cemetery to do prayers. It was that kind of place.

In the monasteries of Tibet, the monks learned only the debate subjects and memorized root texts and commentaries. Each monastery has its own colleges—Sera Monastery has Sera Me and Sera Je, Ganden has Shartse and Jangtse and Drepung has Loseling and Gomang. Each college has its own author for the debate textbooks it uses and that is what the monks study. They also memorize thousands of pages of root texts and commentaries by the Indian pandits and great Tibetan lamas like Lama Tsongkhapa on the five great treatises: Abhisamayalamkara, Vinaya, Madhyamaka, Abhidharmakosha and Pramanavarttika. All twenty-four hours are full.

For example, Geshe Gelek is the resident teacher here at the Kadampa Center in North Carolina and his teacher, Gyüme Khensur Rinpoche Lobsang Delek, is the ex-abbot of the Lower Tantric College. Rinpoche had a couple of nicknames: "Uma Jugpa," which means Madhyamakavatara, or "Entering the Middle Way View," and "Lo Delek," which is also an abbreviation of his name. If I tell you his teacher's story, you will know how intensively many of the monks studied.

In the morning, the monks would get up early and memorize texts. Then they would go to receive teachings from their teachers and afterwards go to the debate courtyard for class debate. After that, the monks would assemble and do prayers to purify, collect merits and pacify obstacles in order to complete their studies, gain realizations and achieve enlightenment. They would do Tara prayers, White Umbrella Deity, *Heart Sutra* and so on. There were also many prayer requests for people who had died or were sick. Then they would continue with one-on-one debate and after that come back for lunch. Then some of the monks would go for more teachings, followed by dinner, private study and many more hours of debate outside in the courtyard.

There were different places for debate. On certain days of the week the monks of all four traditions would gather together on one platform and do puja and prayers together. They would begin with a class, then prayers and afterwards one-on-one debate. The monks from Sera, Ganden and Drepung would debate together and the other traditions could join if they wanted. Sometimes the younger monks would debate until midnight. Some evenings it was like that and other evenings the different colleges would debate in their own places. Sera Me and Sera Je had a place for debate, Ganden Shartse and Ganden Jangtse had another place with different days for debate and prayer, and Drepung Gomang and Drepung Loseling had their own place. Then there was a large platform where everybody could come together for debate.

At nighttime, after finishing hours of debate, Geshe Gelek's teacher would come back, drink some black tea, then put a seat outside his room and recite many of the hundreds of pages that he had memorized. His house was just next door to mine. Behind my bed there was a window and then outside and a little bit to the right of that was his window. Especially he would recite Lama Tsongkhapa's famous text, *The Interpretative and Definitive Meaning, the Essence of Good Explanation,* which introduces the four different philosophical schools' views of emptiness and particularly the Madhyamaka Prasangika School's view. It is a very, very important text and difficult to learn, but he had memorized all those hundreds of pages and recited them by heart many times. He would recite very loudly for several hours till about 3 o'clock. Then he would go to sleep for two or three hours. Not much. In the early morning, he would get up and begin memorizing again. That is just one example of how the monks dedicated their lives to study Dharma. It is most amazing. Maybe that will give you an idea of the rest. There were many other monks who had completely memorized this text, as well as other texts, even in the building where I stayed. I started memorizing it but reached only sixteen pages and then there was an obstacle. I contracted TB and had to go to Darjeeling. I didn't have the merit to complete it.

In Tibet, the monks didn't have to learn how to write. Writing was regarded as a worldly activity, not Dharma. There were many things the monks didn't have to learn. And if a monk started to learn writing, grammar or poetry in the monastery, it was considered that he was taking a worldly life. That is why, when the extremely learned abbots from Tibet came to Buxa and had to sign their names at the Indian office, many of them could not write. They were very famous abbots, very good practitioners, very learned and also great meditators, but they had not learned how to write. I heard that when some of those abbots went to sign their name at the office of the head of the Tibetan Lamas' Camp—a Punjabi Sikh with a very glorious looking moustache and beard who had been a commander in the Second World War—they drew something like a small box or put a thumb stamp.

For many years the abbot of Sera Je at Buxa was Gen Lobsang Wangchug. He had been the abbot in Tibet and was one of the top scholars. Each college has a few very learned and top scholars and he was one of them. The most amazing thing is that in Tibet, when the monks took teachings, they could not write down anything. There was only the mind. Isn't that incredible? They could not write, because most of the monks didn't know how to write, and there were no machines like tape recorders to record the teachings and then listen again afterwards. Everything was up to the mind, how much the mind could grasp. Can you imagine? It was all up to how much you could pay attention and how much intelligence you had. There was no other way to learn. And you have to understand that the subject is not easy; the philosophical subjects are extremely deep and vast. There are so many different views and debates that go deeper and deeper; and they were able to manage with just the mind. These days we have more possibilities to write or record the teachings or even buy the recording from someone else later, but I'm not sure if that causes laziness. In Tibet, there was no laziness. Those great abbots were extremely learned in the philosophical subjects of Dharma, but they didn't know how to write. It is very interesting.

Buxa was an unbelievably hot place and the conditions were really poor, but the monks there put incredible effort into their study of the Dharma. They sacrificed their lives and many became great teachers. Many of those monks have now passed away, but most of the top elder teachers in South India today are from Buxa, like Geshe Gelek's teacher. They are able to educate many thousands of young monks, giving them a very deep, profound and clear understanding of Dharma so that Buddhism can flourish. Every year these monasteries produce qualified teachers, who have finished studying the five great scriptures and completed their examinations. These teachers can then be sent around the world to teach and help many sentient beings meet the Dharma. In the FPMT organization alone there are now forty resident teachers, and there are many others around the world. Many of our resident teachers studied in South India, not Buxa, but they were educated by those monks who came from Buxa. There are now many young dynamic scholars and teachers like Geshe Gelek, who are spreading the light of Dharma more and more in many countries of the world and especially in the West, which has been dark from the beginning.

In the past, there was no light of Dharma in the West—no

knowledge or wisdom about what is right and what is wrong, what is harmful and what is beneficial. Dharma wisdom is not a small wisdom; it encompasses the path to liberation from samsara, the whole Mahayana path and enlightenment. The wisdom . that knows what is right and wrong, and what is harmful and beneficial, is completed only when you achieve the state of omniscience. The reason why we in the FPMT are able to spread the Dharma in this world is because of those monks who studied very hard at Buxa, in that unbelievably hot place, poor and in such bad living conditions. They put incredible effort into studying the Dharma day and night and now we are able to help the world because of that. We are able to enlighten the world and bring Dharma wisdom and light into people's lives, dispelling the darkness of ignorance because of that.

Freda Bedi, Rachel Levy and Sister Vajra

While those other monks who became great teachers were studying so well at Buxa, I just wasted my time. It is not that somebody else caused me to waste my time; my own mind wasted my life. I spent time memorizing English words the same way Dharma is learned by memorizing texts. One time I started to memorize the dictionary, but of course it didn't work. I would forget words and have to go back through and memorize them again. I did that a few times. Lama Yeshe actually copied out the dictionary. There was a thick book of words in Lama's own writing but I don't know where it is now. Lama copied from the first *English-Tibetan Dictionary* composed by Kazi Dawa Samdup of Sikkim, which was printed in Calcutta on very, very bad paper and with binding that broke when you folded it.

Memorizing those English words really didn't help. When I tried to use them people couldn't understand me. For example, Freda Bedi started a school for young lamas twice. The first school was in Delhi and I was there for six months until I had to go and stay in the TB hospital. I tried to learn English while I was in the hospital by going to see an old educated Indian man who I met outside one time while walking. I went to his house a few times taking along a book of Hindi and English given to me by His Holiness Ling Rinpoche's past life's secretary Thubten Tsering. The second school Freda Bedi started was in Dalhousie. She invited me to attend and I went. When I met her, I was talking about His Holiness Song Rinpoche and I said that His Holiness was "doing puja" but I think I used the word "rites," which I had memorized. She couldn't understand me at all and thought I was saying that His Holiness Song Rinpoche was "writing." Eventually she had to ask a translator to come over and help. So the English I learned at Buxa didn't really help. The language I have been speaking all these years is what I have picked up from the students since the time we met Zina.[27]

Anyway, as I mentioned, Freda Bedi found me a pen friend in London, an old lady called Rachel Levy, who was a member of the Buddhist Society. She was a very good lady. After I got TB, she sent the school all the money I needed for medicine, milk and other expenses. At the time, I had no idea who sent the money; it was only much later that I found out it was her. She also gave money to Sister Vajra to make a set of robes for me when I was at Buxa and things like that. That is how I came to find out about Sister Vajra. Most of the letters I had at Buxa were from Rachel Levy. Other people could not read her letters easily because she had an old lady's handwriting. One time she asked me, "Do you want to come to England?" I think she just wanted to check my reaction, to experiment on me. Of course, I answered "Yes." She replied, "When you become like Lama Trungpa, then you can come to England."[28] She was very wise. By the time I eventually

27. Zina Rachevsky, a Russian-American "princess" and Lama Yeshe's and Lama Zopa Rinpoche's first student and nun. See *The Lawudo Lama*, pp. 202 ff.
28. Chogyam Trungpa Rinpoche (1939–87) was a famous Buddhist master who spread the Dharma in the West and created the Shambhala organization. He came

got to England, Rachel had passed away, but I met her cousin and her cousin's husband a few times over the years.

Sister Vajra was ordained by Domo Geshe Rinpoche. Not Lama Govinda's guru—the great yogi who lived in Tibet[29]—but the next incarnation who completed his study for the lharampa geshe in Tibet and was just about to come back to Domo or Yatung in Tibet, which is near Sikkim, when mainland China invaded and Rinpoche was put in prison. The monasteries and all the benefactors from different places were waiting for Rinpoche to return, totally excited and preparing an unbelievable welcome, but it never happened. Eventually Rinpoche was released and he very wisely brought five or six trucks of texts with him to India. In Buxa, there were many difficulties because there were so few texts. The monks had to write out their own texts from the one or two copies available. When Domo Geshe Rinpoche came to Kalimpong bringing various philosophical texts from Tibet it helped the monks a lot.

Originally I was talking about what happened to Sister Vajra but then my story went for a long walk and became a bit of a movie show! Sister Vajra had a nice little cottage in Darjeeling, which I visited. Normally there is a lot of rain in Darjeeling and it is quite foggy. One day a landslide was coming and people shouted to her from outside to get out of the house but she was having some difficulty leaving and I think she was busy packing up her money. Then, just as she was about to come out, the whole house collapsed on her, and she died holding an umbrella in one hand and a briefcase with money in the other. That shows how

---

to England in 1963 on a scholarship to Oxford University and was the first Tibetan to become a British citizen. He taught at the Buddhist Society in Eccleston Square, where Rachel Levy was a member. Lama Zopa Rinpoche first came to England in 1975.

29. Lama Govinda's guru—the previous Domo Geshe Rinpoche Ngawang Kelsang—was made famous by *The Way of the White Clouds*, one of the first popular books on Buddhism published in the West. He founded several monasteries in the Himalayan region, a branch of which Lama Zopa Rinpoche entered as a child. The Domo Geshe mentioned here was born in 1937 and died in 2001.

even shelter—which is supposed to protect life—can become a condition for death.

THE *REAL* MEDITATION IS LAM-RIM

Life is very short and there is not much time left. We can't really tell when death will come because there are so many more conditions for death now than there were maybe a few hundred years ago. Therefore, it is extremely worthwhile to attend this lam-rim course, especially if, like me, your mind is usually preoccupied with so many other things that there is no time to meditate on lam-rim, which is the real meditation. Maybe you are doing tantric meditation because it interests you more, or not doing any kind of meditation, but the *real* meditation is lam-rim, the stages of the path to enlightenment.

The great enlightened being Pabongka Dechen Nyingpo mentioned in his teachings that it is more meaningful to spend our lives meditating on the lam-rim, the three principal aspects of the path, than to recite many hundreds of millions of OM MANI PADME HUM or other mantras.

He also said that it is more meaningful to spend our lives meditating on lam-rim than even seeing the Buddha. Of course, you can understand that you don't get enlightened just by seeing the Buddha and not meditating on the lam-rim. It is not like that. You need to have realizations. The delusions don't all go away just like that. First you must have the realization of guru devotion, the root of the path to enlightenment, which makes possible all the rest of the realizations up to enlightenment. Then you need renunciation to eliminate attachment; right view, or the wisdom realizing emptiness, to eliminate ignorance; and bodhicitta to eliminate the self-cherishing thought. On the basis of that, you have to actualize the generation and completion stages of tantra which purify ordinary death, intermediate state and rebirth into the path-time three kayas—the path-time dharmakaya, sambhogakaya and nirmanakaya. You have to make preparation for those realizations by planting the seed of the three kayas. You need to develop the realizations of the generation stage and then the completion stage. You must achieve all of this in order to be enlightened and it doesn't happen all at once just by seeing the Buddha. Of course, you do receive Buddha's blessing but not all those realizations. That is why Pabongka Dechen Nyingpo Rinpoche says it is more meaningful to meditate on lam-rim than to even see the Buddha himself.

I think that amongst our students there are some who have seen Buddha. Many ordinary people who have great devotion or whose minds are purified see Buddha, but it doesn't mean that they realize bodhicitta or emptiness just by that. You can't even get sutra realizations by seeing Buddha, let alone tantric ones.

Therefore, it is extremely worthwhile to come together and meditate even for two weeks. At home there are many distractions but here we follow the discipline and meditate in a group so that something gets done and preparation is made in the mind to achieve these realizations quicker. Then, sooner or later they will come; if not this life, then for sure in the next. That means it will be quicker to achieve enlightenment. And you can never be sure this is not your last opportunity. OK? You cannot tell.

EVERYTHING DEPENDS ON YOUR ATTITUDE

I thought to start by explaining how to practice normally in daily life and to begin by giving a general understanding of how to start the day.[30]

First, I want to mention something Lama Tsongkhapa explained in his *Mind Training Poem*. I received the oral trans-

---

30. Other practices explained by Rinpoche to be done at the start of the day—such as the morning mantras and bodhicitta mindfulness practices—are included in the appendices. See appendices 1, 3 and 4. More explanation can be found in the FPMT online modules of *Living in the Path*.

mission of this poem from Kyabje Ling Rinpoche in Dharamsala along with Lama Yeshe. That time, His Holiness Ling Rinpoche from his own side also gave us the oral transmission of *The Special Qualities of Lama Tsongkhapa's Teachings* composed by the great Amdo lama Je Gungtangpa and may have given me the text. Lama Tsongkhapa mentioned,[31]

> If you don't purify negative karma and defilements
>   quicker and quicker,
> Being totally under the control of very forceful karma,
> Even though you know this is happiness, that is
>   happiness, you are powerless to choose;
> Even though you know this is suffering, that is suffering,
>   you are powerless to free yourself.
> Therefore, reflect that action and result are non-betraying,
> Look now to choose between white and black karma:
> From this day take care not to create negative karma;
> From this night attend to virtue.
> What better can you do with this life than take care
> Not to create negative karma but instead create virtue
>   all the time?
> White and black actions depend on good and bad
>   thoughts:
> If you have good thoughts, even the paths and grounds
>   are good;
> If you have bad thoughts, even the paths and grounds
>   are bad.
> Everything depends on your attitude.

31. According to Geshe Thupten Jinpa, this *Mind Training Poem* has not yet been translated. The last four lines of the poem are cited by Pabongka Rinpoche in *Liberation* to illustrate the importance of motivation. In *Liberation in Our Hands, Part One*, p. 141, the title of the poem is translated as *Alliterative Poem on Mind Training* or *The Practice of Mind Training Presented in an Ornate Poetic Composition*. In the Tibetan, it is vol. *ba*, p. 773 of Lama Tsongkhapa's *Collected Works*. The verses translated here by Rinpoche comprise roughly a third of the complete poem.

Lama Tsongkhapa is saying that each one of us is totally under the control of very hard, forceful, powerful karma and if we don't purify all of this as quickly as possible, even though we know what is happiness and what is suffering, we are not free to choose. Somehow we just have to go through sicknesses, relationship problems, business problems and whatever other experiences, powerless to immediately free ourselves from them. Once an action is done, karma is created. If the action is non-virtuous, the result will definitely be suffering. If the action is virtuous, the result will definitely be happiness. "Therefore, reflect that action and result are non-betraying" means that these results will definitely come. Therefore, we need to reflect on this and then abandon negative karma and practice white karma, or virtuous action.

Lama Tsongkhapa warns us that we need to take care not to create negative karma, like being careful of the food we eat, protecting ourselves from a poisonous snake or taking care when travelling on a very dangerous road or around anything that is harmful and could cause sickness or death. Then specifically Lama Tsongkhapa says,

> What better can you do with this life than take care
> Not to create negative karma but instead create virtue
>   all the time?

This is what we need to do *all the time.*

> White and black actions depend on good and bad
>   thoughts:
> If you have good thoughts, even the paths and grounds
>   are good;
> If you have bad thoughts, even the paths and grounds are
>   bad.
> Everything depends on your attitude.

Lama Tsongkhapa is saying that everything depends on the mind, everything depends on our attitude. That is something great to learn—how everything depends on the mind.

For example, if you have a bodhicitta motivation, the good heart benefiting other sentient beings, you can actualize the realizations of the Mahayana path, the five paths and ten grounds.

If you *don't* have a good heart, then even if you have renunciation and a realization of emptiness, you can only enter the lower path, the Lesser Vehicle path, and the highest you can achieve is the lower nirvana. That is it. You cannot become a bodhisattva and collect skies of merit in every second with every single action of body, speech and mind, as well as purifying all the heavy negative karmas collected in this and past lives. Without bodhicitta, the good heart benefiting others, you cannot achieve enlightenment and do perfect work without the slightest mistake for sentient beings, liberating every one of them from the oceans of samsaric suffering and bringing them to enlightenment.

Also, the self-cherishing thought makes your attitude bad. It interferes with your achieving the realizations of lower nirvana, the thirty-seven aids to enlightenment and the five paths to liberation. Use yourself as an example: so far, because of following the self-cherishing thought from beginningless rebirths up to now, instead of practicing bodhicitta and benefiting others, you have not been able to achieve the path to liberation or any other realizations. You have not even achieved the very first realization of impermanence and death, which makes the mind become Dharma.

Self-cherishing interferes with your achieving enlightenment and liberating numberless sentient beings in each realm from the oceans of samsaric suffering and bringing them to enlightenment. Not only that; it also interferes with your achieving liberation from samsara, a good rebirth and happiness in all your future lives. The self-cherishing thought even creates many obstacles to your achieving the happiness of this life.

Today's self-cherishing thought doesn't allow your actions right now to become a cause of enlightenment, liberation from samsara or the happiness of future lives. It creates so many obstacles even for the happiness of this life, whether it is travelling, business or whatever. It makes things so difficult. From self-cherishing come attachment to this life, anger and all the other delusions. That is how self-cherishing becomes such a great obstacle for the success of this life. All the obstacles come from the self-cherishing thought.

Creating a bodhicitta motivation for life

Since everything depends on our attitude, the idea here is to start each day with a bodhicitta motivation, not only during this retreat but generally in our practice in daily life.

Two bodhicitta motivations for life are explained here to be used first thing in the morning on waking. The first one, *Cutting the Concept of Permanence* (chapter 3), is from sutra and is longer. The second, *Give Up Stretching the Legs* (chapter 4), is shorter and based on a verse from tantra that His Holiness Serkong Tsenshab Rinpoche would often teach. You can choose either one. After that, there are some verses to be recited—*Bodhisattva Attitude* (chapter 5)—explaining how you are going to dedicate your life to others. They are taken from the great bodhisattva Shantideva's *Guide to the Bodhisattva's Way of Life*. There are elaborate and shorter versions of these verses, so again you have some choice depending on time.

3. Cutting the Concept of Permanence[32]

Bodhicitta Motivation for Life 1

CUTTING THE CONCEPT OF PERMANENCE

Start by thinking:

> Guru Shakyamuni Buddha descended into this world
> from Tushita Pure Land and showed the twelve deeds
> of a buddha. He taught the Dharma by expounding
> the 84,000 teachings and enlightened numberless sen-
> tient beings not only in this world but also in other
> universes. In this way, the benefits to sentient beings
> were as limitless as the sky.
>
> In the general view,[33] the Buddha turned the Wheel
> of Dharma three times. He taught the four noble truths
> in Sarnath, the middle Wheel of Dharma revealing the
> *Perfection of Wisdom Sutras* at Rajgir and the final
> Wheel of Dharma teaching the three characteristics
> at Vaishali. Then he manifested into Buddha Vajra-
> dhara and deities to reveal the tantric teachings. He

32. This commentary is based on *Light of the Path*, 9 September (evening) 2009. It is supplemented by material from the Chinese New Year motivations of 14 February 2010 and 3 February 2011, Amitabha Buddhist Centre. See also *Teachings from the Medicine Buddha Retreat*, ch. 2.

33. In the view of ordinary beings the Buddha did these actions, but for those with a higher view, the Buddha's actions are beyond ordinary comprehension.

manifested into Chakrasamvara and revealed the Chakrasamvara teachings on the top of Mt. Meru, into
Yamantaka at Orgyen in Pakistan and into Kalachakra
at Amaravati in India.

Finally, the Buddha showed impermanence to us
sentient beings and passed away into the sorrowless
state. All that is left now are scriptures and some ruins
at holy places like Rajgir and Sravasti. Therefore, there
is no question that I myself can die even today.

Actually, it is best to think, "I am going to die today." Or to
actually decide, "I *am* going to die today." That is an even better
antidote to the concept of permanence that doesn't allow you to
practice Dharma.[34] It cuts the concept of permanence that doesn't
allow your actions to become the cause of enlightenment, liberation from samsara or even the happiness of future lives. It cuts
the attachment to this life that makes your actions only nonvirtue
and doesn't allow them to become Dharma, which brings happiness beyond this life.[35]

The problem is that our minds are always taking the side of the
concept of permanence. It is like in the government of a country;
there are always two parties, left and right wing. In the United
States, there are Democrats and Republicans. Usually, people like
me live our lives toward the concept of permanence and *that* is
the problem. When you live life with the concept of permanence,
attachment, worldly concern and all the other negative emotions

34. The concept of permanence in this context is the thought "I am going to live
for a long time." It "doesn't allow" us to practice Dharma because it obscures
our minds from seeing that the nature of life and all causative phenomena is
impermanent. This means that we become attached to the appearance of this life
and constantly go after short-term pleasures, delaying and always putting off our
Dharma practice. (*Three Principal Aspects of the Path*, 27 February 2011).

35. Actions done out of attachment seeking only the happiness of this life may or
may not bring the result of happiness this life, but they are always nonvirtuous.
Lama Atisha explained this to his disciple Dromtönpa. See *Door to Satisfaction*,
p. 18 ff. and *Light of the Path*, 13 September 2010.

arise. Then your mind becomes a problem and life becomes hard. Life becomes difficult.

Equalizing the eight worldly dharmas

There are so many problems when you live life with attachment and worldly concern. You want comfort and happiness and therefore suffer and become unhappy when there is discomfort. You look for a good reputation, wanting many people to say good things about you, and suffer when that is not happening or the opposite happens and you have a bad reputation. You grasp at praise, wanting other people to say good things to you, and your mind goes down when that doesn't happen or you are criticized. You grasp at receiving things and are disappointed when nothing comes. First, you advertise your birthday to other people, then when you don't receive any gifts or birthday presents from your friends, your mind goes down, down, down and you become depressed and unhappy.

These problems come because the mind is grasping. It is the mind *grasping* at comfort and pleasure, reputation, praise and receiving material things that is the root problem. It is because the mind is grasping that there is dislike and unhappiness when the things you want don't happen or the opposite happens. Nagarjuna's advice was to equalize these thoughts: [36]

> Receiving and not receiving material things, comfort
> and discomfort,
> Good and bad reputation, praise and criticism—
> Equalize these eight worldly dharmas
> And banish them from your mind.

36. *Nagarjuna's Letter*, v. 29. For more explanation of this verse, see *Door to Satisfaction*, especially chs. 3–5 and *How to Practice Dharma*, ch. 2. The definition of the best Dharma practitioner is one who has equalized these thoughts. (*Three Principal Aspects of the Path*, 27 February 2011.)

If you check the nature of your mind when it is grasping at these things, it is not peaceful but disturbed by emotional thoughts. There is no inner peace or calm. Grasping at these four objects of desire is a big problem in our lives and all our other problems come from that. But when these four pairs are equalized and there is no more thought of the eight worldly dharmas, you have real inner happiness, the happiness of Dharma.

Asanga explained the difference between samsaric pleasure and the happiness of Dharma in eleven points that are mentioned in the Kadampa teachings. For example, that samsaric pleasure is extremely small while Dharma happiness is unbelievably great and that samsaric pleasure is only in the nature of suffering while Dharma happiness is real happiness.[37]

When your mind is living in Dharma with the thought of impermanence—that death is going to come today—you don't have all the problems that most other people suffer from. You don't have to go and discuss those problems with psychologists

---

37. Rinpoche explains Asanga's eleven points contrasting worldly and Dharma happiness as follows. The worldly pleasure that comes from following desire, such as eating, drinking, (enjoying) women (or men), singing and dancing has the following drawbacks: (1) it doesn't satisfy the whole body; (2) it depends on outside conditions and therefore only happens sometimes and not whenever we want; (3) it doesn't exist in all three realms—the form, formless and desire realms; (4) it is not a cause to achieve the seven treasures of the aryas; (5) the pleasure is finished by enjoying it; (6) it can be cut short by our enemies; (7) it cannot be carried into future lives; (8) it cannot be completed—worldly pleasure never brings real total satisfaction; (9) it is the cause of all the suffering of this and future lives; (10) it is a "pleasure" that is merely labeled on a base that is actually suffering—like a leper calling the relief from scratching an itching sore "pleasure"; (11) it causes attachment and delusions to arise; these then propel us to engage in negative karmas such as killing, stealing, sexual misconduct, lying and so forth. The happiness of Dharma, on the other hand: (1) satisfies the whole body; (2) happens whenever we want it; (3) exists in all the three realms; (4) causes us to achieve the seven treasures of the aryas; (5) never finishes and always increases; (6) cannot be destroyed by enemies; (7) is carried into future lives; (8) can be completed and brought to full satisfaction; (9) generates no suffering in this or future lives; (10) is not merely labeled on a false base—like calling pieces of cut-up newspaper a "million," "billion" or "zillion dollars"; (11) destroys all the delusions. (From Lodrö Gyaltsen's *Very Beginning Mind Training Opening the Door of Dharma; Light of the Path,* 22 September 2010.)

and other professionals, which makes life very expensive. Being a friend of attachment and the concept of permanence—which is not true—and living life that way, brings a whole package of problems. Life becomes filled with one problem after another, exactly like it's shown on TV or in the movies.

Now when you live with Dharma, by thinking of impermanence and death, you free yourself from all these problems. Freeing yourself from the concept of permanence, attachment and so forth means also freeing yourself from anger and all the problems that come from anger, such as jealousy. You free yourself from all those sicknesses and chronic diseases of the mind and open the door to peace. It is amazing. You give yourself peace and from that great inner peace come a healthy mind and a healthy body. That's how it works. Your healthy Dharma mind makes your physical body healthy also.

Wow! Then it saves you a lot of money. Your healthy Dharma mind living with the thought of impermanence immediately cuts out many unnecessary activities and expenses, and then the money you have left can be used for meaningful things that benefit yourself and others. All the unbelievable expenses that go to feed attachment to this life, the thousands and tens of thousands and hundreds of thousands and millions and billions spent for the emotional mind, are cut. Can you imagine? You spend an unbelievable amount of money for attachment—which is a wrong concept and in nature a disturbing thought—and for the self-cherishing thought, while the money you spend to benefit other sentient beings sincerely from the heart, for your enlightenment, liberation or even for the happiness of your future lives is very little.

This is just a slight elaboration to help you see life more clearly. Like using a telescope to see something very far away or a microscope to see atoms or tiny sentient beings, similarly, here you use the Dharma to see your life and go beyond. By using Dharma wisdom you can see what is mistaken and what is correct; what is useless and what is useful; what is meaningless and what is meaningful; what is to be abandoned and what is to be practiced; what brings suffering and what brings happiness. It is all to do with the mind. It all depends on your attitude, which way you think, whether you live with your mind in the concept of permanence or impermanence. It makes a huge difference to your life, like the difference between the earth and the sky. It is amazing! When your mind is living in the concept of impermanence suddenly you no longer have all those hundreds of thousands of problems.

Next think:

> Then there were the two close disciples of the Buddha, Shariputra and Maudgalyayana; the Six Ornaments, the pandits Nagarjuna, Asanga, Chandrakirti and so forth; and many other great Indian yogis such as Naropa, Tilopa and Saraha. They wrote many texts, taught and gave unbelievable, incredible benefit to sentient beings and to the teachings of the Buddha in this world. Now we can only hear their names and see the texts they left and some caves and places where they meditated and achieved realizations. Therefore, there is no question that I myself can die even today.
>
> After that, many great lamas appeared in each of the four traditions in Tibet, including Padmasambhava and Longchen Rabjampa; Marpa and Milarepa; the five great Sakya pandits; Lama Tsongkhapa and his disciples, and so forth. They completed the path to enlightenment and gave incredible benefit to sentient beings and to the teachings of the Buddha. Now we cannot see them, just the places where they practiced, like the caves of Lama Tsongkhapa and Milarepa, and their texts, nothing else. They all passed away. Therefore, I myself can die even today.

Now think of all the virtuous friends you have met, like Lama Yeshe who was kinder than all the numberless past, present and future Buddhas. In the past we were able to receive teachings from Lama and like the sun shining he gave incredible great benefit to this world, to sentient beings and to us. Lama was so entertaining as well. He brought such extremely worthwhile entertainment and incredible joy. Now that aspect doesn't exist.

Then, Kyabje Ribur Rinpoche, those who received teachings and initiations will remember him; Kyabje Serkong Tsenshab Rinpoche, for those who had the great fortune to receive teachings from him a long time ago; and Kyabje Song Rinpoche, the great, great pandit, scholar, highly attained yogi and enlightened being. Many virtuous friends came, but now we cannot see them.

Think particularly of those virtuous friends with whom you made a Dharma connection and who have passed away. Now those aspects no longer exist. So here think of your gurus who have passed away and think, "Therefore, I myself can die even today." Each time you think of death like this, cut your attachment.

Now think of your family members who have passed away. Think of your father and mother if they have passed away. Then think of all your friends and the people you knew who have died and think, "Therefore, I myself can die any time. I can die even today."

Then there were so many people born on the same day as you in this world, who were the same age, and who have already died. Think of them and contemplate, "Therefore, I myself can die even today."

The very beginning of Dharma: the thought of impermanence

When you have in mind the thought that death can come today, if something suddenly happens, it is not a shock. It is not a shock at all because your mind is prepared. You have already trained your mind by thinking very strongly about death first thing every morning and keeping that awareness throughout the day. That helps you to be at peace and not have fear when you face a life-threatening problem or something similar.

If your mind has not become Dharma because you haven't trained in the thought of impermanence but instead have always thought, "I am going to live for a *long* time," and done all your activities with attachment to this life, then if something opposite to that suddenly happens and the reality of life—its imperma-nence—is shown, all of a sudden, while you are planning billions of things, you get an incredible shock.

You may know Buddhism and have memorized the hundred volumes of the Buddha's teachings (*Kangyur*) and the two hun-dred volumes of commentaries (*Tengyur*) and be able to explain and recite them by heart, *but* your mind has not thought about impermanence. You may know by heart all the root texts, the five great treatises, along with the tantric texts and commentar-ies and be able to explain them, *but* your mind has not thought of impermanence. Because you have been living your life with the concept of permanence, the day something happens and the reality of life is shown, it is a shock and there is incredible fear. Suddenly you see that you don't want to die. It is not that you don't want to die because you want to benefit sentient beings. I am not talking about that. You don't want to die for fear of what will happen after death. You don't want to die *because of fear*. You don't want to lose this body. You don't want to lose your possessions, property, belongings or family. Your mind is clinging to these things and because of that, there is great fear.

Meditating on impermanence is the very beginning of Dharma, but look what happens if this meditation is left out or if you thought it wasn't important because emptiness, shunyata or some tantric meditation was more important.

Of course, if you already have the realization of impermanence, then it's different. [After that, you can realize emptiness and with the realization of emptiness][38] you see things as an illusion and like a dream. You see yourself, actions, possessions, family and people around you like a dream or an illusion. You are like a person who can recognize a dream as a dream. There is a big difference between someone who can recognize they are dreaming while they are dreaming and someone who cannot and believes everything is true. There are huge differences between their lives. For people who can recognize a dream as a dream, nothing that happens while they are dreaming bothers them because they know it is not true. Even if somebody praises them as the best of the best, they know there is nothing to be attached to because it is not true. And no matter how badly somebody criticizes them or puts them down—even down below the ground—they know there is nothing to be upset about because it is not true. Like that, everything is seen as like an illusion, a dream or a reflection.

It is like watching a movie and believing that what you are seeing is true. If, instead of understanding it is just a series of pictures, you believe that real people are being killed in a war, a real house is falling down or a car is just about to have a real accident, you will be very nervous and frightened. Or it is like seeing the reflection of a face and believing it to be a real face. There is a huge difference between seeing a reflection and knowing it to be a reflection and not knowing it is a reflection and believing it to be a real face. Like these examples, those who have realized emptiness and trained their minds in that see everything as an illusion or a dream.

So even though meditation on impermanence is the beginning of the gradual path of the lower capable being in the lam-rim, can

---

38. Rinpoche does not actually mention realizing emptiness at this point. I have added the words in brackets to clarify the following paragraph, which is describing what happens after the realization of emptiness, not impermanence.

you imagine how important that realization is? The Kadampa
geshes used to say:

Even though you have a hundred qualities, because
you are under one mistake, no realization happens.

A "hundred" means "many," like the *Hundred Devas of Tushita,*
which doesn't mean that there is literally a fixed number of only
a hundred devas in Tushita and there can't be more, but is an
expression of there being many or numberless. What the Kadampa
geshes were saying is that you may have a lot of understanding
and education and know thousands of millions of things, but
everything gets stuck because of one mistake. Why is your mind
not subdued, why have you not had any realizations of the path
to enlightenment and why have all your daily activities—eating,
walking, sitting, sleeping, working and, of course, meditating
and studying Dharma—not become Dharma, even though you
have so much knowledge and know so many things that your
mind is full? It is all because of one mistake—not thinking about
impermanence and death. Because of not reflecting on impermanence and death, no matter how much meditation or retreat
you do and no matter how much Dharma you study, nothing
becomes Dharma. None of your virtuous activities become holy
Dharma. Therefore, there is no question that all your ordinary
activities of eating, walking, sitting, sleeping and working do not
become Dharma. Everything becomes worldly dharma but not
holy Dharma. It is like that.

One thing is that nothing becomes Dharma that can benefit
you at the time of death and bring happiness beyond this life. The
other is that, because there is no realization of impermanence and
death, the gradual path of the lower capable being is not there.
Because that is lacking, there is no realization of the gradual
path of the middle capable being. And because that is missing,
there is no realization of the gradual path of the higher capable

being. Therefore there is no bodhicitta, and without bodhicitta, tantric realizations cannot be achieved. When the realization of impermanence and death is missing, none of these paths can be completed.[39]

That is why, when you don't think about impermanence and death, no matter how much knowledge or education you have, all the same problems arise as if you didn't know Dharma. Even if you have studied all the five major sutra texts, their commentaries, and tantra, and even if you have extensive knowledge and are able to explain this and that, because the very beginning practice of impermanence from the gradual path of the lower capable being is missing, it is like you don't know Dharma. You have all the same problems as somebody who is not a Buddhist and has not studied Dharma. When you encounter a problem, there is no difference between having met Dharma and learned everything and not having met Dharma and not knowing anything. It is the same. Your mind is no different.

What I am saying is that if the mind training in the meditation of impermanence is missing, look how much danger your life is in! There is no difference between a person who has met and studied Dharma and somebody who has not, between somebody who is a Buddhist and who is not, between somebody who has studied the philosophical or lam-rim teachings extensively and who has not. It is like that.

You have to understand the point: sometimes there could be *even more* problems. Sometimes a person who has met Buddhism

39. The paths of the three capable beings are explained at the beginning of Lama Atisha's *Light of the Path*. Usually they are translated as the "lower, middle and higher scopes," but Rinpoche comments: "This is an old translation from the very early days in Dharamsala and not exactly what Lama Atisha said. The Tibetan is *kye-bu sum gyi lam-gyi rim-pa*. *kye-bu* means 'capable' and when you leave out that word you lose the whole entire meaning. It should be translated as 'the graduated path of the three capable beings' but *kye-bu sum*, 'three capable beings,' is left out. 'Capable beings' has great meaning. It is the main subject of the lam-rim, the path to enlightenment; therefore, this must be translated exactly." For a summary of the three paths, see *Door to Satisfaction*, pp. 19–22.

could have even more problems than one who is not a Buddhist, because although there is greater education and more learning, the basic practice has not been done, and since the basic practice is missing, the problems could be even bigger.

I elaborated quite a bit here to introduce the subject of impermanence, but when you do the meditation it can be condensed.

So many times I have almost died

Then think:

> So many times already in this life, I have almost died. I have almost had a fatal car accident or a fall. Somehow death has not yet come, but if I had died already, by now I would be in the lower realms.
>
> By now, I could be a fish caught by a fisherman with the hook in my mouth, unable to escape and in unbelievable pain. Even before I was completely dead, my body would be sliced in half.
>
> By now, I could be a worm pierced by a bird's beak and carried off half-dead. Or I could be a worm attacked and covered by hundreds of ants biting my body. There would be nothing I could do.

Even if one ant bites your foot, it is very unbearable, but a small worm doesn't have thick skin. There is no protection when it is covered by hundreds of ants. By now, you could be born like that.

> By now I could be in those most terrifying hell realms.

This could happen because you have collected so many causes to be born in the lower realms since beginningless rebirths and they are not yet purified.

Therefore, right now I *must* abandon negative karma,
the cause of suffering, and practice only virtue, the
cause of happiness.

Bring it to this conclusion: "I *must* abandon negative karma and
practice only virtue."

Death can come any moment

After that, think as Nagarjuna explained in the *Precious
Garland:*[40]

Life is like a butter lamp in a strong wind; (it can stop
any time.)

"This life—*my life*—is like a candle or a butter lamp outside in
the wind." The flame is blown this way and that, and can go out
any time. Think, "My life is like this; it can stop any time. Death
can come any moment." Meditate on that.

Also think of Nagarjuna's quotation:[41]

This life is more impermanent
Than a water bubble blown by the wind.
How wonderful it is to be able to wake up from sleep
(The fragile state of) simply breathing in and out!

When you go to sleep, the senses are not functioning. It is like
dying. You are just breathing in and out. Recently, Geshe Sopa
Rinpoche used this quotation in a motivation to teachings on
the wisdom chapter of *A Guide to the Bodhisattva's Way of*

40. *Buddhist Advice*, p. 136, v. 317. This and the following quotation can be
found in *The Great Treatise on the Stages of the Path to Enlightenment, Volume
I*, p. 156.
41. *Nagarjuna's Letter*, p. 80, v. 55.

Life, and said, "You breathe out and stop breathing in and that's it. You've gone." You're finished just by that. Therefore think, "How wonderful it is to have the freedom to be able to wake up from sleep!"

Then think:

> Last night many people in this world died. They went to bed with so many plans for things to do tomorrow, this year, next year and so on. This morning their bodies were corpses.

That happened to so many people in the world last night, not just one. Can you imagine?

> If I had died last night, by now I would be in the lower realms, in those most frightening hell realms, because although I did study Dharma and do some practice and retreat, I didn't engage in continual intensive Dharma practice.

From time to time we did do some practice, but then anger, ill will and many other things destroyed the merits we created. There are many things besides anger that can blow up our merits. Anger, ill will and heresy all destroy them, and pride weakens them.

> Therefore, there was no really serious, continual, pure Dharma practice and purification. If death had come to me last night, by now I would be in the hell realms.

THE GREAT MEANING OF THIS HUMAN LIFE

It is a miracle to be able to wake up in the morning with a human body. Compared to the number of beings who are born in the lower realms, those who are born human are very, very few. The number of sentient beings who are born in the hell realms, for example, is unimaginable. It is like the number of particles of dust on this great earth. The number of beings born as pretas is like the grains of sand in the Pacific Ocean. The number of beings born in the animal realms is like the blades of grass in this world. While the number of beings born in the higher realms is very few. Those who gain a perfect human rebirth are like the grains of dirt that are caught under your fingernail when you scratch the earth.

Sentient beings are born in the hell realms due to attachment, anger and ignorance and the negative actions these delusions cause them to create. It is unbelievably rare to gain a perfect human rebirth because the causes are so difficult to create. To gain a human rebirth depends upon creating good actions motivated by a pure mind of non-ignorance, non-attachment and non-anger. It also depends on having practiced pure morality—abstaining from killing, lying, sexual misconduct and so forth. Keeping pure morality is extremely difficult. First of all, it is difficult for sentient beings to understand and accept the need to abstain from these actions. Then, it is difficult to take a vow to do so. Finally, even if the vow is taken, it is difficult to keep it purely because there are so many obstacles from within and from outside.

For these reasons, it is extremely rare to be reborn as a human being and even rarer to gain a precious human rebirth with all the eighteen qualities needed to practice Dharma, the eight freedoms and ten richnesses. Therefore, think:

> How most unbelievably fortunate it is that I have the freedom to wake up and practice Dharma. In every second there is so much I can do with this human body, not only a precious human body so extremely rare to find, but one with eighteen qualities almost impossible to achieve again. Wow!
>
> In each second I have the great freedom and opportunity to create the cause to achieve happiness in all my

future lives by generating renunciation of this life.

Not only that, in each second I also have the opportunity to create the cause to achieve ultimate happiness, liberation from samsara, by generating renunciation of future lives and actualizing the right view.

Not only that, in each second I have the great freedom and opportunity to create the cause to achieve enlightenment by generating bodhicitta.[42]

The ability to create the cause of all this temporary and ultimate happiness even in one second is the third great meaning of life.[43] Therefore, think:

Each second of this perfect human rebirth is much more precious than mountains of gold and diamonds, or gold and diamonds the size of this earth.

Not only that, it is more precious than even one wish-granting jewel.

If you put a wish-granting jewel on top of a banner on the fifteenth day of the Tibetan month, you can receive whatever external enjoyment or necessity you want just by praying for it. That is why a wish-granting jewel is the most valuable external material thing, more precious than anything else. But this perfect human rebirth that we have is much more precious than the whole sky filled with wish-granting jewels. The value of all that

42. This reflection can be expanded to include the tantric path by adding: "Not only that, by practicing tantra I can achieve enlightenment in one lifetime, while by practicing Highest Yoga Tantra I can achieve enlightenment within one brief lifetime of this degenerate time or even within a few years."

43. The three great meanings of this precious human rebirth are its great value (1) in a temporary sense because it can be used to attain a future rebirth in higher realms or a pure land, (2) in an ultimate sense because it can be used to achieve liberation and enlightenment and (3) even in each moment. See *Liberation, Part Two*, pp. 80–84.

is nothing compared to this perfect human rebirth, because even if you owned skies filled with wish-granting jewels, without this perfect human rebirth you could not achieve the happiness of future lives, liberation from samsara or full enlightenment for sentient beings. Therefore, every second of this perfect human body is so precious.

You must try to *feel* how this perfect human rebirth is most precious. After that, think:

> Therefore, I must not waste even a second of this life!

Wasting even a second of this life by not practicing Dharma is a greater loss than wasting all those other precious things.

> I must make it meaningful by practicing Dharma.

What does it mean to practice Dharma? Normally I explain it this way: One meaning is practicing the three principal aspects of the path to enlightenment, the heart of all Buddha's teachings—renunciation, bodhicitta and right view—as a foundation. Then, on the basis of that, the generation stage of tantra, abandoning impure appearance and impure thought, or whatever you are able to do.

Another explanation of practicing Dharma is living in vows, the three levels of vows—pratimoksha, bodhisattva and tantric. Living in the pratimoksha vows doesn't mean everyone has to become a monk or nun. If you are lay, it means living in the lay vows.

GENERATING BODHICITTA

Then think,

> Since I am going to die today, what should I do?

The answer is "bodhicitta."

I *must* practice bodhicitta.

Bodhicitta is the very essence of Dharma and the best way to make this life meaningful. By praying never to separate from bodhicitta during birth, the intermediate state and death your practice becomes a part of the five powers to be practiced near the time of death[44] and also makes a connection with the advice for integrating the whole lifetime into the five powers.[45]

Now reflect on the shortcomings of cherishing the self, which opens the door to every suffering and obstacle, and on the benefits of cherishing others,[46] which brings all the happiness up to enlightenment to you and to numberless other sentient beings, as well as every quality.

You can do this by reflecting in the following way: If you have a bodhicitta motivation, the good heart benefiting other sentient beings, you can actualize the realizations of the Mahayana path, the five paths and ten grounds. You can become a bodhisattva and collect skies of merit in every second with every single action of body, speech and mind. You can purify all the heavy negative karmas collected in this life and past lives and achieve enlightenment for sentient beings. Then you can do perfect work without the slightest mistake for sentient beings, liberating every one of them from the oceans of samsaric suffering and bringing them to enlightenment.

---

44. The five powers to be practiced near the time of death are: (1) virtuous practice—to purify and distribute wealth; (2) intention—a positive frame of mind; (3) countering negativity; (4) prayer—never to separate from bodhicitta and not be overcome by the delusion of ignorance; (5) acquaintance—assuming the lion position. See *Practicing the Five Powers near the Time of Death*.

45. The five powers to be integrated into the whole lifetime are: (1) intention; (2) virtuous practice; (3) countering negativity; (4) prayer—dedication; (5) acquaintance. For more on these two sets of the five powers, see *Liberation, Part Three*, pp. 186–90.

46. A summary of this is given in the next two paragraphs based on a passage from chapter 2. See also appendix 6.

But if you follow the self-cherishing thought, you can't do this. Self-cherishing interferes with your actions becoming the cause of enlightenment, liberation from samsara or even the happiness of future lives. With self-cherishing, there are many obstacles to achieving even the happiness of this life. It makes things so difficult. All obstacles come from the self-cherishing thought.

Taking away the suffering of others

Now do the practice of exchanging self for others[47] along with the practice of taking and giving (*tong-len*). While you are doing taking and giving, you can chant the mantra OM MANI PADME HUM.

First, do the practice of taking by generating compassion for the numberless sentient beings suffering under the control of delusion and karma. Then take on their sufferings and the causes of those sufferings, delusion and karma, along with even the subtle defilements.

For example, when you are taking on all the sufferings of the hell realms, there are: the suffering of the place—e.g. the whole ground filled with swords or completely on fire, the burning red-hot iron houses, huge cauldrons and extremely hot molten hard-iron;[48] the actual sufferings; and the cause of those sufferings, delusion and karma, along with even the subtle defilements.

Take all of this into your heart and give it to the self-cherishing thought, like putting a bomb on top of your enemy and completely destroying it. Meditate a little that the truly existent I,

47. This can be done by thinking, "Up to now I have always regarded myself as most important and precious. I have neglected others and put my own interests and welfare first. Now I am going to regard others as most important and precious. I am going to put the interests and welfare of others first and neglect my own." In this way the attitude viewing oneself as most important is exchanged for the attitude that sees others as most important and all the energy that previously went into cherishing the self is instead directed to others.

48. Tib: *khro-chu*. This is not just the usual molten iron but an extremely hard type of iron that has melted because it is so hot. (Most Secret Hayagriva Retreat, 14 March 2010.)

the real I that the selfish mind cherishes but which is not actually there, becomes totally non-existent even in name.

Then take on the sufferings of the numberless hungry ghosts, animals, human beings, suras, asuras and intermediate state beings. The taking can be done in an elaborate, medium or short way by taking all the sufferings together; it just depends on time.

You can also take on obstacles. If your gurus have taken the aspect of having sickness, you can take on any obstacles to their actions to benefit others according to the karmic view of sentient beings. When it says in the teachings that there is nothing to be taken from the gurus, it means that they do not have obstacles and sickness the way that ordinary sentient beings do, but there *is* the karmic view of sentient beings that sees obstacles, sickness and so on.[49] After that, you can take on all the obstacles to the spreading of the teachings of the Buddha because it is from these teachings that sentient beings receive all their happiness up to enlightenment. Finally, you can expand your meditation to take on the obstacles to the benefactors who serve the Dharma and the Sangha.

Giving every happiness to others

When you are doing the practice of giving, first generate loving kindness and then give to each hell being, hungry ghost, animal, human, sura, asura and intermediate state being, either one by one or all together. Give all your past, present and future merits; the results of these merits, all the temporary and ultimate happiness up to enlightenment; and all your material possessions, including all the money you have in the bank, your car, purse and all your family and friends.

49. From the viewpoint of the practice of guru devotion, since the gurus are enlightened beings, they have no causes to experience sickness or obstacles. Therefore, when our gurus appear to be sick or have obstacles, it is simply the view of our own impure mind. This impure karmic appearance of sentient beings is what is to be "taken" in the practice of taking and giving.

Think that by receiving these things, the numberless sentient beings receive a perfect human body, meet the Dharma and meet a virtuous friend. They gain perfect enjoyments, perfect companions and their environment transforms into a pure land where there is no suffering and only beauty. It is filled with wish-granting trees that fulfill all their wishes and even the wind blowing through the trees, the animals and birds make the sound of Dharma. It is incredible.

Think also that what you give them becomes the realizations of the complete path to enlightenment in all their hearts, which liberates them from all the oceans of samsaric suffering along with its causes, delusion and karma, including the subtle defilements. By this, they all achieve the unimaginable qualities of a buddha and become the deity you are practicing.

Giving can also be done in an elaborate, medium, short or very short way according to time. Each time you do the practice of taking and giving you create unimaginable merits and become closer to enlightenment, which means closer to liberating numberless sentient beings.

Concluding prayers

After that, think:

> This is just visualization. In reality sentient beings are still suffering. I must liberate them from the oceans of samsaric suffering along with its causes, karma and defilements, and bring them to enlightenment by myself alone. Therefore, I must achieve enlightenment. Therefore, I am going to engage in virtuous activities.

"Virtuous activities" refers to whatever virtuous practices you are going to do, such as reciting *sadhanas*, meditation, preliminary practices or meditating on the lam-rim. It is also very good to dedicate all the ordinary activities of eating, walking,

sitting, sleeping and working that you are going to engage in by
thinking:

> May all my activities of body, speech and mind become
> the cause to achieve enlightenment and to enlighten all
> sentient beings.

And you can pray:

> From now on, may I be like Lama Tsongkhapa, by
> having the same qualities, and may I be able to offer
> limitless skies of benefit to sentient beings and to the
> teachings of the Buddha.

It is very good to pray like that at the end.

This is what to think first thing in the morning when you wake
up. This is your motivation for life. It is not just for today but
from now on. Here I elaborated the section on impermanence;
you can condense it when you do the meditation.

There is another shorter motivation based on His Holiness
Serkong Tsenshab Rinpoche's teachings, *Give Up Stretching the
Legs* (chapter 4). It uses a quotation from tantra to set the motivation when you wake up. So you have a choice sometimes to
do this motivation and sometimes to do the other one.

After either of these motivations, there are some verses to
recite from *A Guide to the Bodhisattva's Way of Life*, explaining
how to dedicate your life from today until you die. (See *Bodhisattva Attitude*, chapter 10.)

4. Give Up Stretching the Legs[50]
Bodhicitta Motivation for Life 2

His Holiness Serkong Tsenshab Rinpoche would always mention this practice to be done in the morning upon waking. It is another way to generate a bodhicitta motivation and is based on a concise but very effective quotation from tantra. Although it is just a four-line verse there is a lot to meditate on within each word.

In tantric practice there is sleeping yoga without creativity, or mental fabrication, and sleeping yoga with creativity. Sleeping yoga without creativity means that either you go to bed meditating on the dharmakaya or you go to sleep meditating on emptiness. Sleeping yoga with creativity means that instead of falling asleep in the state of emptiness, you visualize yourself as the deity in the mandala and so forth, and go to sleep with that pure mind remembering the guru-deity.

Then, the next morning on waking, you rise up from the state of clear light to the sound of the dakas and dakinis playing music and saying this verse:

> Give up stretching the legs.
> Give up entering samsara.

---

50. This commentary combines *Light of the Path*, 10 September (afternoon) and 11 September (evening) 2009. It also draws from Most Secret Hayagriva Retreat, 6 March 2010, and 7 October 2010, Shedrup Ling.

Generate bodhicitta to achieve Vajrasattva,
the Great Victorious One, for all sentient beings.[51]

GIVE UP STRETCHING THE LEGS

"Give up stretching the legs."[52] That is a very good expression!

51. The Tibetan for this verse is

Kang-pa kyang-pa pang-nä-ni.
Kor-wai ngag-zhug dor-nä-su.
Dor-je Sem-pa Gyal-po-che.
Yang-dang yang-du kul-war-ja.

Although the original has four lines, Rinpoche usually uses only the first three and that is why the fourth line is omitted here and in the commentary. It can be translated in various ways. In the Most Secret Hayagriva Retreat, Rinpoche roughly translated it as:

Having abandoned stretching the legs,
Give up looking at samsara as good and engaging in it,
Generate bodhicitta to achieve enlightenment for sentient beings.

In Shedrup Ling:

Give up stretching the legs,
Give up being attracted to samsara,
Achieve enlightenment for sentient beings.

An older and alternative translation of the verse by Rinpoche and Basili Llorca— which includes all four lines—is in the Heruka retreat instructions, *The Good Vase of the Dakinis' Secret Treasure Nectar:*

Abandon stretching out the legs,
Give up serving samsara.
Vajrasattva, the great Victorious One.
Persuades us again and again.

The source of the verse is not clear; however it is mentioned in the Heruka Body Mandala commentaries of Pabongka Rinpoche and Trijang Rinpoche as the advice given to the great mahasiddha Luipa by Heruka. For an older and alternative teaching on these verses, see "Four Fundamental Retreats," *Heart Advice for Retreat*, pp. 41–68.

52. *Kang-pa kyang-pa pang-nä-ni.* "Give up stretching the legs." This line contains all the meditations of the path for the lower capable being: perfect human rebirth, death and impermanence, suffering of the lower realms, refuge and karma. Here it is clinging to this life and being too lazy to practice Dharma that is to be given up. Rinpoche is not saying you can't stretch out your legs to go to sleep at night, but don't be lazy and put off practicing Dharma thinking it doesn't matter and that there is plenty of time, because that's not true.

When your mind becomes lazy you stretch out your legs, then you stretch out your whole body in the ten directions. Whatever you can, you stretch out. There is no rush to practice. Goodbye Dharma! This life and this moment's happiness are more important. It is not expressed in words but physically that is what is being manifested. There is no thought of how sentient beings are suffering and the need to help them by practicing Dharma and becoming enlightened. That is why this line is saying,

> Give up clinging to this life and being too lazy to
> practice Dharma.

Because that is what happens when your mind is in that state. Therefore,

> Instead, think of impermanence, which is the nature
> of this life.

Death is definite and it can come any time. It's not that your life is permanent by nature but you need to think of it as impermanent. No! The nature of your life *is* impermanent and if you believe it to be permanent you get into trouble. You get into very long term trouble and have to remain suffering in samsara. There is no enlightenment, no liberation, no happiness in future lives and no happiness or success even in this life. All the actions of your body, speech and mind become negative karma because everything is done out of attachment to this life and is therefore non-virtuous. This most precious human body is totally completely used for negative karma and then you have to be born and suffer in the lower realms.

This human body qualified with eight freedoms and ten richnesses is most unbelievably precious. Right now, you have met the Buddhadharma and you have met a guru. With this body you can purify all the negative karmas collected from beginningless time that cause rebirth in the lower realms and you can create all the causes for happiness in future lives as well as ultimate happiness, liberation from samsara. You can even achieve the peerless happiness of great liberation, full enlightenment, and then liberate numberless sentient beings from the oceans of samsaric suffering and bring every one of them to full enlightenment. You can do all this with a human body qualified with the eight freedoms and ten richnesses. For example, Milarepa didn't have even one single rupee or dollar, he only lived on nettles, but he had a precious human body and by practicing Dharma he achieved enlightenment within a few years of that life.

Therefore, our human body is amazing and precious. It is highly meaningful but difficult to find again. Although we have received it this one time, it won't last long because its nature is impermanent. Death is definite and can come any time and any moment, even today, and at the time of death, nothing can help except the holy Dharma. After death there are only two possible rebirths—in the lower realms or in the body of a happy transmigratory being. There is no third option. Where we reincarnate depends on karma. Birth in a lower realm is the result of negative karma; a higher rebirth is due to good karma. Good karma comes only by practicing Dharma.

So far in this life, even though some of us met the Buddhadharma many years ago, the karma we have collected is mostly negative. Even in one day we collect mostly negative karma and the negative karmas we collect are very powerful because the four parts of the action—the base, intention, action and dedication—are more complete. Even when we do practice Dharma, these four are not usually complete. Often the motivation or dedication is missing and therefore the actions are weaker. It means that if death were to come now, definitely we would be born in the lower realms, and once we are born there, we have to remain until the karma for that rebirth finishes.

A year in a hell being's life is very long and the length of life of a hell being in even the very first of the eight major hot hells, Being Alive Again and Again, is around two trillion two hundred and sixty billion years.[53] That is an unbelievable, unbelievable number of human years. In the next hot hell, the Black Line, the lifespan is twice as long and the suffering is even greater; and so it goes on.

Once you are born in the first hot hell, you have to remain there until the karma finishes, then another negative karma ripens bringing another suffering rebirth in the lower realms, and it goes on like that. It is not sure when you can come back to the human realms. That is very difficult to say. There is no opportunity to practice Dharma in the lower realms because you are totally overwhelmed by suffering. You cannot achieve the happiness of future rebirths, liberation from samsara or enlightenment. You can neither benefit yourself nor others. Therefore, *right now,* while you have this perfect human rebirth qualified with the eight freedoms and ten richnesses, which is so precious and so difficult to find again, it is not the time to be "stretching the legs." You must practice Dharma and you must practice right away.

GIVE UP ENTERING SAMSARA

"Give up entering samsara"[54] means:

> Give up thinking that samsara and samsaric pleasures are good and then clinging to them.

53. Rinpoche gives the number of years as two great *tra-trig*, two great *ter-bum*, then six *ter-bum*. One *ter-bum* is 1 billion. Ten *ter-bum* (10 billion) is a great *ter-bum* (*ter-bum chen-po*). Then ten great *ter-bum* (100 billion) is one *tra-trig*. Then ten *tra-trig* (1 trillion) is a great *tra-trig*. See LamaYeshe.com for a complete table of Tibetan numbers.

54. *Kor-wai ngag-zhug dor-nä-su.* "Give up admiring and entering samsara." Rinpoche explains that *ngag* has the meaning of praising or admiring samsaric pleasures, thinking over and over again how wonderful they are, looking at them as being real happiness and then being attracted to them. Because of that wrong view, we enter (*zhug*) or engage in samsara. Therefore, what is to be given up here is the

Instead, realize samsara to be suffering as in reality it is
only suffering.

Because of always looking at samsara and its pleasures as real,
pure happiness, thinking how good they are and admiring them,
attachment rises and then we enter and engage in samsara. This
is what needs to be given up by thinking how samsara is only in
the nature of suffering.

What is samsara?

It is very important to be aware of what samsara is, otherwise
you won't know exactly what you want to be liberated from
and there can be a lot of misunderstanding. Samsara is not this
earth, the houses, factories or even Disneyland. It is not even
exactly this body and mind; these aggregates. Samsara means
"circling" *(khor-wa)* and that refers to the continuity of these
aggregates. Lama Tsongkhapa explained in the *Great Treatise*
that samsara is:[55]

The part of the continuity of the contaminated aggregates caused by delusion and karma.

The Tibetan is *zag-che nyer-len gyi phung-pöi gyun-gyi-cha. Zag-
che:* "the contaminated seed of delusion"; *nyer-len:* "caused by
delusion and karma"; *phung-pöi gyun-gyi-cha:* "the part of the
continuity of the aggregates."

Zag-che is the "contaminated seed of delusion." Here the word
used for "delusion" is *zag* in Tibetan and it literally means "to

---

mind that views samsaric pleasure as happiness instead of viewing it as suffering,
which is the reality. This line contains all the meditations of the middle capable
being: contemplating how samsara is only suffering, understanding the cause of
samsara and generating the path to liberation.
55. I have not managed to locate this in the *Great Treatise*. However, there is a
similar definition of samsara in *Liberation, Part Three*, pp. 2–3.

fall down." If you have delusion you always stay in samsara and you can never achieve liberation. You "fall down" to the lower realms, then you are reborn in the higher realms, then the lower realms, over and over like this. What is being expressed here is that the aggregates are "contaminated" by the seed of delusion. They are contaminated because they contain the seed of delusion and from that seed, delusion arises. Delusion then motivates karma, which plants a karmic seed on the mental continuum that throws us into future rebirths. The seed of delusion compounds the suffering of the mind and body this life. It also compounds future rebirths and future lives' sufferings. That is why these aggregates and all six realms are pervaded by suffering. The desire, form and formless realms[56] are all pervaded by suffering; they are in the nature of suffering. The contaminated seed of delusion is in the nature of suffering and therefore the aggregates are pervaded by suffering. That is what is being described in "pervasive compounding suffering."[57] It is the seed of delusion that *compounds* the sufferings of both this and future lives. The aggregates are also pervaded by suffering because they are caused by delusion and karma; therefore the body and mind are in the nature of suffering.

Pung-pöi gyun-gyi-cha is "the part of the continuity of the aggregates." Here, the word "part" is used to express that the continuity of the aggregates ceases for a meditator who has attained the path of meditation. There are five paths: the path of merit, the preparatory path, the right-seeing path, the path of meditation and the path of no more learning. When a meditator attains the

56. The six realms are contained within the three realms of desire, form and formlessness.
57. In this paragraph, Rinpoche is explaining pervasive compounding suffering, which is the third of the three types of suffering in samsara and the main suffering to be understood in order to appreciate what samsara is and what it means in Buddhism to achieve liberation. Pervasive compounding suffering is the foundation for the other two sufferings (the suffering of pain and the suffering of change) and by freeing ourselves from that the other two sufferings are ceased and liberation is achieved.

path of meditation, his or her aggregates will no longer continue to circle to a future life; the continuity has ended. That meditator still has samsara[58] but by achieving the path of no more learning, the aggregates will not continue to the next life because delusion and the cause, or "seed," of delusion—the negative imprint—are ceased. Therefore, there is nothing to reincarnate and nothing to cause reincarnation. The word "part" refers to the aggregates of the meditator who has attained the path of meditation. For the rest of us, who have not achieved this, who have not ceased the seed of delusion and whose aggregates will continue to circle to the next life, there is no need to say "part of the continuity..." just "the continuity..."

Nyer-len means "caused by delusion and karma."[59] To understand this, you have to think about the twelve dependent related limbs, then you can see how all this is caused by delusion and karma. Delusion and karma are the main causes.

His Holiness the Seventh Dalai Lama and Kyabje Pabongka Dechen Nyingpo describe samsara as:[60]

The part of the continuity of the *birth* of the contaminated aggregates caused by delusion and karma.

Kyabje Denma Lochö Rinpoche also explains it that way. This is the precise meaning of samsara; the name is given according to the function of the action of "continuity" or "circling." When the

58. The meditator still has samsara because he or she still has the samsaric aggregates they were born with. That is what the word "part" refers to. Once those aggregates cease, no new aggregates will be produced and they will achieve the state of no more learning—passing into the state of nirvana. This seems to be referring to meditators on the Lesser Vehicle path.

59. Rinpoche's translation here and above is not literal but thought provoking. A more literal translation of *nyer-len gyi phung-po* would be "aggregates (which are products) of (karma and) delusions." The aggregates (*phung-po*) arise from the afflictions and—as Rinpoche goes on to explain—by implication karma is involved. Pabongka Rinpoche explains that the aggregates are connected to the afflictions in three ways, see *Liberation, Part Three*, pp. 2–3 and notes, pp. 40–41.

60. *Zag-che nyer-len gyi phung-pöi kye-wäi gyun-gyi-cha.* See note 55 above.

continuity of these contaminated aggregates caused by delusion and karma taking birth again and again is stopped—wow! *Then* liberation from samsara is achieved. This happens *only* by ceasing the causes, delusion and karma. Pabongka Dechen Nyingpo says that these samsaric aggregates are not the actual samsara; it is the action of this continuity that is what samsara really is.

By understanding what samsara is, you can see how it is only in the nature of suffering.

Samsara is only suffering

All the suffering in samsara is of three types: the suffering of pain, the suffering of change and pervasive compounding suffering. It's very important to meditate on these because then you can realize how samsara is in the nature of suffering.

The suffering of pain—heat, cold, hunger, thirst and so on—is easy to understand, even animals can recognize this as suffering and don't want to experience it. The heaviest suffering of pain is experienced in the lower realms but even in the human or deva realms where there is samsaric pleasure still it is only in the nature of suffering, it is the suffering of change.

The suffering of change includes all samsaric pleasures. We label pleasure on what is really only suffering. We merely impute pleasure and then it appears back to our hallucinated mind as real pleasure, real pure happiness, but that is completely wrong, it is totally non-existent. There is a very good verse in the *Guru Puja* to help us realize that samsara and its pleasures are only in the nature of suffering. It talks about the mistake of viewing samsara as "a very beautiful, happy park":[61]

> Samsara is extremely unbearable like a prison;
> Please bless me to give up looking at it as a very
>   beautiful, happy park.

61. V. 88.

Because of totally believing that samsara and its pleasures are real happiness when in reality they are real suffering, we become attached to them and that ties us to samsara with the chain of the twelve dependent related limbs and causes us to be continuously reborn in samsara and experience suffering. It is like taking poison with the total belief that it is medicine and having to continually experience many unwanted suffering results including death as a consequence, but not realizing that this suffering is the result of a wrong concept. Or it is like walking over a cliff because of wrongly believing there is a real path there, then falling and being injured and dying, but being unable to see that it came from a wrong belief.

Samsaric pleasure is only suffering because it is labeled on the feeling of relief when a previous suffering that was heavy has stopped and a new suffering is beginning from small. "Pleasure" is labeled on that feeling, but it doesn't last. It is not like Dharma happiness, which can be developed and completed.[62] The more samsaric "pleasure" is continued, the more it decreases and becomes the suffering of pain again. Every samsaric pleasure is like that, whatever base it is labeled on, whether it is the pleasure of sleeping, the pleasure of playing music, the pleasure of eating food, the pleasure of sex or whatever.

When a previous suffering, which was great, stops, the action compounding the next suffering begins. While that suffering is still small it is unnoticeable and is labeled pleasure, but as it increases the pleasure goes away and it becomes the suffering of pain. It is because the pleasure is labeled *on* the feeling of suffering that it doesn't last. First of all, samsaric pleasure doesn't increase, unlike Dharma happiness, which can be fully developed. Second, it doesn't last. Even the pleasure that is generated doesn't last because it is suffering. We have to understand this well.

Lama Tsongkhapa explained the suffering of change very

62. See note 37 contrasting samsaric happiness and Dharma happiness.

clearly in the *Great Stages of the Path to Enlightenment.*[63] For example, when the body is exposed to the hot sun there is a feeling of suffering. On entering the cold water of a river, swimming pool, lake or ocean, there is a feeling of relief because the previous suffering of being hot that was great ceases. But the action of entering the water starts another suffering of being cold. At the beginning, since one suffering has stopped and the next suffering is small, that feeling is labeled "pleasure." But after some time, as it continues, it becomes unbearable; it becomes the suffering of pain again.

It is the same with eating. First the action of not eating compounds hunger. Then when you start the action of eating, the previous suffering of hunger stops from being great and the new suffering of eating begins. The discomfort starts immediately you begin eating but because it is unnoticeable that feeling is labeled "pleasure." That is why, as you continue eating, the pleasure you experienced at the beginning is no longer there. As you eat a second plate, a third plate and so on—depending how big your stomach is!—it changes and becomes more and more uncomfortable.

Sometimes the food might be very salty but when you start eating it is not noticeable. The first plate of food is OK but when you get to the second plate you feel, "Oh, this food is really salty!" I am telling you this from my own experience. It is interesting because you cannot taste the salt at the beginning so I am not sure which plate you regard as being salty and which non-salty? Anyway, as you continue to eat you realize there is too much salt.

There are many other examples, even sleeping. First you think, "Sleeping is so comfortable." But although sleeping for eight hours may be possible, if you try to continue sleeping for twenty-

63. *The Great Treatise, Volume One*, pp. 291–92. Lama Tsongkhapa does not use the specific example that Rinpoche gives here, but there is a similar example in *Liberation, Part Three*, p. 39.

four hours, two days, three days or a week, after some time you get bored. The pleasure doesn't increase and doesn't last. As the action continues it becomes the suffering of pain. That shows that it is not real happiness. The "pleasure" is merely labeled on a suffering feeling.

All samsaric pleasure is like this. At the beginning it is OK, but after some time it gets boring; it is the suffering of change. That is why worldly people change their lives so much going from one trip to another trip because they cannot get satisfaction. Whatever they do it is not real happiness, so they get bored and keep changing.

Of course in the West, generally karma can change and people begin to look for a spiritual life, an "inner" or "truthful" life. In the past, they could not find satisfaction and had many problems, and now they look for something meaningful and worthwhile. There are people in the West whose minds are quite sharp and even without hearing any Dharma, they cannot find any meaning in the life they are living. People have told me that they always found life meaningless; they always felt something was missing and were never happy until they met the Dharma.

Of course, if you are not living your life with compassion and benefiting others, even if you are a billionaire, trillionaire or zillionaire, it is totally meaningless. But if you have a good heart and are serving others, even if you have no religion and haven't met the Dharma, there is meaning to your life. Since you are creating good karma, there will be happiness for others and happiness for you in the future. As a result of even one act of kindness you will experience happiness for many hundreds of thousands of future lifetimes. You may not be doing anything to free yourself from the prison of samsara, from the oceans of samsaric suffering and its causes, delusion and karma, but if you have a good heart and are helping others, there is meaning to your life. And if you are wealthy and using your wealth to help others, there is meaning to that. Otherwise there is nothing, just an empty life, like an empty container. All your actions of body, speech and mind—your whole life from morning to night, from birth to death—become only negative karma. It is a very sad life. Even when you try to attain pleasure, it is only for yourself. Therefore it is a very sad life.

So give up being attached to samsara and its pleasures, wealth and enjoyments, by realizing that they are all only in the nature of suffering. As the *Guru Puja* says, "Samsara is extremely unbearable like a prison; give up looking at it as a very beautiful, happy park." Give up the attachment to samsaric pleasures that arises by thinking, "How good this is, how good that is . . ." because that continuously ties you to samsara. It is like chaining yourself to a huge block of wood that is blazing with fire and then getting attached to the chain. It is because of being attached to samsara and its pleasures, that we have been suffering from beginningless rebirths up to now, taking birth and dying again and again in samsara and experiencing all the sufferings in each of the six realms, as well as the intermediate state. That is how our lives have been from beginningless rebirths up to now: *totally* under the control of delusion and karma. We have never had a break from the suffering of samsara for even one second. I am not only talking about this life but from *beginningless* rebirths up to now. Up to this second, we have never had one moment or one second's break, holiday or vacation from the suffering of samsara. Not one.

It doesn't mean that we have been constantly experiencing the suffering of pain. I am not saying that. It doesn't mean that we have been experiencing the suffering of change continuously without break. I am not saying that either. It is the third type of suffering, pervasive compounding suffering—which is the aggregates—that we have never had a break from up to now. As His Holiness the Dalai Lama often says, these aggregates are pervaded by suffering being under the control of delusion and karma and that is why this body and mind are in the nature of suffering all the time. The desire, form and formless realms are all like that.

In the desire realm there are all three types of suffering. The form realm doesn't have the suffering of pain but according to Geshe Sopa Rinpoche they "might" have the suffering of change. The formless realm doesn't have the two other sufferings, but it has pervasive compounding suffering. In the formless realm there is no body—just the mind—but still the aggregates are caused by delusion and karma, so they are in the nature of suffering. The philosophical texts and the lam-rim mention that because the aggregates of the formless realm contain the contaminated seed of delusion, they are pervaded by suffering.

First, understand the meaning of "pervasive," then understand the meaning of "compounded." It is very good if you can understand the Tibetan. *Khyab-pa* means "pervasive," *du-je* is "compounded." The seed is compounded for us here in this life; it compounds our physical and mental suffering. As I mentioned before, it also compounds our future lives' rebirths and suffering. Therefore, these aggregates are "pervasive compounding suffering" (*khyab-pa du-je kyi dug-ngäl*).[64]

So "give up entering samsara" by realizing that samsara, its pleasures and perfections—wealth, reputation, enjoyments and all these things—are only in the nature of suffering. Give up looking at samsara as good and samsaric happiness as real happiness, instead of looking at it as suffering. Remember the quotation from the *Guru Puja* about looking at the extremely unbearable prison of samsara as a "very beautiful, happy park" and bring

---

64. Rinpoche's comment: "Normally this is translated only as 'pervasive suffering' but that is not a complete translation of the Tibetan. There are quite a few things in English not translated exactly according to the Tibetan because many of the translations are from the very early times in Dharamsala. Now people have become familiar with those terms and everybody uses them, but they are not exact. It is very good to translate exactly according to the Tibetan even though it may sound a bit awkward in English. There is a very rich meaning if you translate each word. If you know the commentary, then a few words give the whole view."

it here. Because of attachment to samsara and its pleasures, we have suffered from beginningless rebirths up to now and why we are still suffering is because of *that*.

How samsara cheats us

Samsaric pleasure is very deceptive. It is like a friend who always says nice things but in reality is totally cheating you. To your face that person always praises and says how fantastic you are, but behind your back he is stealing your things and using them; then he kills you.

Remember the story of the cannibals. You find yourself in a land where there are many cannibals and at the beginning the cannibals say lots of nice things to you. They tell you how much they like you and how if you leave them they will suffer unbelievably, they will be so unhappy and sad. They talk like this, blah, blah, blah, and you believe them, thinking you will be safe if you stay there, you will be really happy and things will turn out well. Then once you trust and have decided to live with them, they eat you.

It's the same when you trust and get attached to samsara and its pleasures. A mouse sees food in a trap and runs inside, lured by the pleasure of the food, only to get trapped. A fish sees a worm wriggling on a hook and hurries toward it, lured by the pleasure of something to eat, only to get caught with the hook in its mouth, which causes unbelievable pain, and then sliced and gutted while still alive. Moths see the flame of a candle as something very beautiful and fly into it, only to be instantly burned and enveloped by wax. That is what happens when you are attached to samsaric pleasure thinking it is wonderful and good; the result is only suffering.

Take the example of alcoholics. They look at drinking alcohol as being real pleasure instead of seeing that it is only in the nature of suffering. In reality, drinking is the suffering of change because the pleasure it brings doesn't continue and doesn't increase. Because they look at drinking as good, attachment arises and they get addicted. It destroys their whole life. Drinking harms them and their family, the wife or husband and children. It wastes so much money and causes so many problems. They suffer unbelievably but can't stop.

This is without talking about all the negative karma that is created by drinking. According to a student who worked in a hospital in the United States, people who are alcoholics usually experience a very heavy death with a lot of suffering. Then, after death they will have to suffer for an unimaginable amount of time in the lower realms. Even if they are again born human due to some good karma ripening after a long time, because of the previous addiction they do the same thing again. Again they become alcoholic and again they waste their whole life, unable to practice Dharma. And so it goes on and on like this for hundreds of thousands of lifetimes: suffering in the human realms and then the lower realms over and over again. The same sufferings and the same problems are experienced endlessly. They can never be free until they purify, practice Dharma and abandon the negative habit of drinking.

The world is full of examples showing how if you get attached to samsara and its pleasures thinking they are real happiness, you are totally cheated and suffer. In meditation, use as many of these examples as possible to get a clear understanding of the need to give up thinking samsara is good and engaging in it. This is very, very important. With this way of thinking, you can continuously practice Dharma. Otherwise, even if you try to practice, it doesn't really become Dharma, a cause to achieve liberation; it just becomes another cause of samsara because the motivation is attachment.

By looking at samsara, which is in the nature of suffering, as being in the nature of suffering, and looking at samsaric happiness, which is the nature of suffering, as being suffering, you are not cheated. You are not deceived by your attachment and your actions do not become a cause of samsara. Then you can be free from samsara and achieve liberation.

Being in samsara is totally scary

The *Guru Puja* says,[65]

> Disturbed by the extremely violent waves of delusion
>   and karma,
> Attacked by the many sea monsters of the three kinds
>   of sufferings—
> Please grant me blessings to generate a very intense
>   strong wish to be liberated
> From this very terrifying great ocean of samsara with
>   no beginning.

Samsara is like a great ocean and delusion and karma are like the extremely violent waves that disturb the ocean. Because of that, there are many sea monsters[66] of the three types of suffering constantly attacking and harming us. This is what being in samsara is like. There is no happiness. We are constantly being harmed by the suffering of pain, samsaric pleasure—which is the suffering of change—and pervasive compounding suffering. Therefore, we ask the *Guru Puja* merit field to grant us blessings to give rise to "a very intense strong wish to be liberated from this very terrifying great ocean of samsara with no beginning."

65. V. 87.
66. Tib: *chu-sin.* I am using the word "sea monster." Rinpoche says: "*chu-sin* means water lion but here it could be whales, I am not exactly sure. It is used as an example for the three types of suffering—the suffering of pain, the suffering of change and pervasive compounding suffering."

We have been experiencing the suffering of samsara from beginningless time, and if we don't practice Dharma, the suffering will have no end.

Also any suffering or problem we are experiencing now is nothing new. This is not the first time. And any samsaric happiness or pleasure is nothing new. Remember that. It may be something new for this life but, whether it is suffering or pleasure, you have experienced it numberless times in the past. Whatever each individual thinks of as being samsaric pleasure, whether it is a relationship or going to the moon with a rocket or without a rocket! Whatever the pleasure is, this is not the first time; we have experienced it numberless times from beginningless rebirths. The problem is that, because of looking at samsaric pleasure as real happiness and being attached to it, we have died and taken rebirth, experiencing the suffering of each realm, numberless times. It is just that most of us cannot remember it. Those whose minds are more purified and have developed reliable clairvoyance through calm abiding or tantric realizations by achieving the *Six Yogas of Naropa* can see all this.

For example, when Lama Atisha took the aspect of being sick and having diarrhea, his disciple Dromtönpa, the embodiment of the Compassion Buddha and one of the previous incarnations of His Holiness the Dalai Lama, cleaned it with his own hands. Dromtönpa offered service without the slightest thought that the holy kaka[67] was dirty and with full devotion that Lama Atisha was a buddha. The guru devotion teachings mention that because of his devotion, he was suddenly able to read the minds of not only human beings but also ants and other small insects and creatures up to the distance it takes an eagle eighteen days to fly. Suddenly he could read everyone's mind very clearly. There are many other stories like that; it didn't only happen to Dromtönpa. And, of course, the guru is the most powerful object.

---

67. Rinpoche's comment: "In the Lhasa dialect there is an honorific word for the kaka of holy beings, *so-gya,* but I'm not sure about holy pipi, or urine."

As your mind is purified, gradually you are able to remember the past and also see many hundreds of thousands of lives into the future. It happens more and more as you actualize the five paths and ten grounds. It is most amazing. You can remember all the experiences of thousands, billions and zillions of past lives. You can remember being in the lower realms and you can remember experiencing the most unbearable sufferings in the human realms. Wow! Then you can't stand being in samsara for even a second. It is like being in the very center of a fire or sitting naked on a thorn bush or on the tip of a needle—there is no happiness or peace at all. You want to get out right this second. It is just that we can't remember.

Our minds are so blocked, so obscured, that we can't see all the unimaginable sufferings of past lives and we can't see that we will have to go through all the same sufferings of the six realms again in future lives. Not just for one future life, but for numberless future lives. Wow! Being in samsara is totally scary. Reincarnating again in samsara is totally scary. Like a prisoner trapped in his cell, when you realize how most terrifying it is to be in samsara even one more second, you won't want to be imprisoned for even a minute or a second longer. You will only want to be free. To be in samsara is unbelievably, unbelievably sad.

Therefore, give up admiring samsara and then entering and engaging in it, because attachment to samsara and its pleasures is what sets off the cycle of the twelve dependent related limbs. As long as you admire and are attracted to samsara you are always cheated by your hallucinated mind, by attachment and ignorance—the concept of true existence. Then you experience the suffering of samsara endlessly, not only from beginningless rebirth but endlessly. Being in samsara is an extremely serious matter. Remember the verse from the *Guru Puja*:

> Samsara is extremely unbearable like a prison;
> Please bless me to give up looking at it as a very beautiful,
>   happy park.

By keeping the treasure store of the arya beings' wealth,
the three higher trainings,
May I hold the banner of liberation.

First we request blessings to be able to give up samsara by no
longer "looking at it as a very beautiful, happy park." Then we
request blessings to apply the antidote by practicing the path of
the three higher trainings, "the treasure store of the arya beings'
wealth."[68] Finally, we ask blessings "to hold the banner of liberation," which means to achieve liberation. This verse has a very
rich, fantastic meaning.

GENERATE BODHICITTA TO ACHIEVE
VAJRASATTVA, THE GREAT VICTORIOUS ONE,
FOR ALL SENTIENT BEINGS

This last line is the special motivation to practice tantra, to achieve
the unified state of Vajradhara or full enlightenment in the quickest way possible for sentient beings. His Holiness Serkong Tsenshab Rinpoche explained that Vajrasattva, the Great Victorious
One (Dorje Sempa Gyälpoche), has both an interpretive and a
definitive meaning.[69] The rough meaning of this is:

---

68. These are the seven treasures of arya beings—faith, ethics, study, generosity,
shame, conscientiousness and wisdom. The principal wealth of the aryas is the
three higher trainings.

69. Buddhist texts often have different levels of meaning. The definitive meaning
is the one that is no longer open to interpretation. The definitive and interpretive
meanings of Vajrasattva the Great Victorious One (Dorje Sempa Gyälpoche) are
not clarified here; instead Rinpoche gives us a rough meaning to work with: "Generate bodhicitta to achieve enlightenment for all sentient beings." Why Rinpoche
translates it this way can be understood by referring to an earlier commentary:
"The 'vajra' in Vajrasattva refers to the unification of the vajra holy body and vajra
holy mind of the Vajradhara state and 'sattva' refers to bodhicitta, the altruistic
thought that wants to achieve that state. And 'the great king' refers to the tantric
path. Vajrasattva, the unification of the vajra holy body and vajra holy mind, is
not separate from the altruistic mind of bodhicitta." See "The Four Fundamental
Retreats," *Heart Advice for Retreat*, p. 62.

Generate bodhicitta to achieve enlightenment for all sentient beings.[70]

The Kadampa teachings explain the reason for doing this:

I is the root of all negative karma; it is to be instantly thrown very far away.
Others are the originator of my enlightenment; they are to be immediately cherished.[71]

Give up the I

The I is like a very dangerous and immediately lethal poison or like garbage.[72] Therefore, it is something to be "instantly thrown very far away." Here I added the word "instantly"—meaning without even a second's delay—because I think it is more exact. You can also think the way it is normally explained in the lam-rim:

70. *Dor-je Sem-pa Gyal-po-che.* Literally, "Vajrasattva, the Great Victorious One" (see explanation above). This line contains all the meditations of the path for the higher capable being contained in the Mahayana Sutrayana and Mahayana Vajrayana. Here it is the I—self-cherishing and self-grasping—that is to be given up and the special bodhicitta motivation for practicing tantra that is to be generated.

71. *Dag-ni lä-ngän tsa-wa-te*
Gyang-kyi kyur-wäi chö-chig-yin.
Zhän-ni jang-chub jung-kung-te,
Chang-te len-päi chö-chig-yin.
The Tibetan uses the term "phenomenon," *chö-chig-yin,* in both phrases; I have changed this to "it" and "they." Rinpoche has adapted the slogan and personalized it by using the word "my." The original can be found in Lama Serlingpa's *Leveling Out All Conceptions,* see *Mind Training,* p. 196, v. 7.

72. It is not exactly the I but self-grasping and self-cherishing that are dangerous and to be thrown far away. In the next paragraph, Rinpoche goes on to explain how we grasp at a truly existent I that doesn't exist and this is the I that we cherish more than anyone else. There are many reasons why this obsessive concern with oneself at the expense of others is harmful (see appendix 6). This doesn't mean we should hate ourselves or lack self-esteem, rather we need to understand that cherishing this I that doesn't exist gives rise to negative emotions and negative actions and suffering—that is why it is the "root of all suffering." For more on this, see chapter 6, *Four Wrong Concepts.*

I is the root of *all suffering*; it is to be instantly thrown
very far away.

Also, you must understand that the I you are cherishing is not
actually there. The I that you think is more important than numberless sentient beings and buddhas is not actually there because
that I is the truly existent I, existing from its own side, which
doesn't exist. So there is nothing to cherish. This is what we have
to remember when we do the practice of taking and giving in
daily life.

Even if it was the merely labeled I that you were cherishing,
which does exist but is empty, still there is no logical reason why
it is more important than anyone else, any other person or insect.
That is just the ego's trip. There is no logic or proof; it is just the
ego's dictatorship.

The great bodhisattva Shantideva says,[73]

If you don't give up the I
Your suffering can't be stopped
Just as if you don't get rid of fire
The burning can't be stopped.

Therefore, to pacify your own sufferings
And to pacify the sufferings of others,
Give yourself up for others
And cherish others as yourself.

This is the total solution and method to pacify your own suffering and the suffering of other sentient beings, who are number-

73. *Guide*, ch. 8, vv. 135–36. This quotation from Shantideva is taken from a talk
by Rinpoche on *Give Up Stretching the Legs*, 7 October 2010, Shedrup Ling.
The full commentary to the third line given during that teaching can be found in
Service as a Path to Enlightenment, pp. 5–17. See also "The Third Power: Blaming
the Ego," *Practicing the Five Powers near the Time of Death*.

less. Give yourself up to others and cherish them as yourself. This is the attitude we need to practice Dharma and this is the attitude to have when working at a center, in a company, in the government and in the family. Cherish others and think of others as yourself.

Cherish others

Others are the originator of my enlightenment; they are
to be immediately cherished.

When the Kadampa masters say that others are the originator of your enlightenment, they are not only talking about your friends or people you like. "Others" doesn't refer to only an animal you like, maybe a cat or a dog, a butterfly, snake, ant or cockroach. "Others" means *every* sentient being: numberless animals, insects, cockroaches, mosquitoes and bugs. It includes all those creatures people are scared of, like rats and scorpions, and every single animal, big or small, as well as all the creatures that live inside our body. It includes numberless hell beings, numberless hungry ghosts and numberless human beings. "Others" means every single human being, however they look and however they act, whether positive or negative. It includes every sura, asura and intermediate state being. "Others" means every single one of the numberless beings in each realm.

When you think of "others," start by looking at everybody around you right now. Then relate it to every insect, every bird and every worm that you see on the road when you go outside. All these "others" are the originator of *your* enlightenment. The Tibetan says "they are a phenomenon to be immediately taken." This is an expression of the Kadampa geshes. To "immediately take something" means to "cherish it." If there were some poo-poo and some wish-granting jewels, you would throw away the poo-poo but immediately seize and cherish the wish-granting jewels. Similarly, the I is like poo-poo to be immediately thrown away, while "others" are like the wish-granting jewels. Therefore, the numberless sentient beings are to be immediately cherished, cared for and served with your body, speech and mind. They are to be freed from suffering and brought all happiness, especially the happiness of future lives, liberation and enlightenment.

"Others" means not just one but all sentient beings and it can have the meaning: "Even if they get angry with me, criticize or abuse me, don't like me, don't love me, always look down at me and always complain about me no matter how much I try to help them or how hard I work." Whatever story you may have about them—that their way of thinking is bad or their manner harmful—*still* they are the originator from whom you receive enlightenment. No matter what they do, they are always the originator of your enlightenment. So it is unbelievable; it is incredible!

And you have to understand that it is not only enlightenment that you receive from others. The numberless sentient beings without exception are also the originator from whom you receive all your numberless past, present and future happinesses.[74] In other words, you receive the happiness of all future lives, liberation from samsara, full enlightenment and every temporary happiness right down to the smallest comfort in a dream from every single sentient being. When you think of sentient beings as the originator of your enlightenment, remember all these other levels of happiness as well. Even if you only think of enlightenment—

---

74. How is it that sentient beings are the originator of all our happiness? In the talk at Shedrup Ling cited above, Rinpoche explains that all our happiness comes from virtue and "our virtue is Buddha's action." Buddha in turn can only come into being by depending on sentient beings because "Buddha comes from a bodhisattva, a bodhisattva comes from bodhicitta, bodhicitta comes from great compassion and great compassion is generated by depending on the existence of suffering sentient beings." Therefore, all our happiness can be seen to have arisen due to the kindness of every single sentient being. In fact, each sentient being is the source of all our happiness because without them there would be no Buddha, Dharma and Sangha. See *Service as a Path to Enlightenment*, p. 8.

what better gift is there than that? A piece of cake?! Maybe when you are very hungry, a piece of cake or a banana is more important than enlightenment!

Next generate bodhicitta by thinking:

> Therefore, in my life there is nothing to do except cherish other sentient beings, work to free them from all suffering and its cause and bring them to enlightenment by myself alone. Therefore, I must achieve full enlightenment.

After that, think:

> From my side, to bring each and every single sentient being to enlightenment, even if I need to be born in the hell realms and suffer . . .

For how long? For eons! For how many eons?

> . . . for eons equaling the number of drops of the ocean or atoms of this earth, I can do that. But from the side of sentient beings, they would have to suffer for an unimaginable, unimaginable, most unimaginable amount of time.

You can't stand how long they would have to suffer. It is too much:

> Therefore, they need to be liberated from the oceans of samsaric suffering and brought to enlightenment as quickly as possible. Therefore, I need to achieve enlightenment as quickly as possible.

This is the special tantric motivation *Dorje Sempa Gyälpoche* to achieve enlightenment, the unified state of Vajradhara in the quickest way. Then think the same way I mentioned previously:

> Therefore, from now on I am going to do all the virtuous activities as well as eating, walking, sitting, sleeping, working and so forth, to achieve enlightenment for sentient beings, to liberate them from the oceans of samsaric suffering and bring them to full enlightenment.

Then pray to be like Lama Tsongkhapa. After that, there are some verses from *A Guide to the Bodhisattva's Way of Life* as a motivation. There is a long and short version so it depends which one you want to do (see *Bodhisattva Attitude,* chapter 10).

5. Bodhisattva Attitude[75]

How to Dedicate Your Life to Others

The verses in chapter 1 are from the great bodhisattva Shantideva's *Guide to the Bodhisattva's Way of Life,* and are to be recited first thing in the morning after you have generated a bodhicitta motivation for life. They explain how you are going to dedicate your life to others by cultivating the bodhisattva attitude. We need this kind of attitude in order to open our minds toward others when working at a center, in the family, in the office, in the government and everywhere. If you can generate this motivation in the morning and then try to live in it throughout the day, your life will become really wonderful. This is the best practice.

It is very good to recite all the verses if you can. If not, you can recite the shorter version, which is the last three verses, from "Like a wish-granting jewel," or the last two, from "Just like the sky."

Giving

I shall give away fully with no sense of loss
My body, enjoyments and all merits of the three times
    (past, present and future)
To accomplish the work for all sentient beings.

75. This commentary is drawn from four teachings by Rinpoche: *Light of the Path,* 10 September (afternoon and evening) 2009; Most Secret Hayagriva Retreat, 14 March 2010; Chinese New Year, 14 February 2010, Amitabha Buddhist Centre; 21 October 2010, Shedrup Ling.

The "work" to be accomplished for all sentient beings is the happiness of this life and all future lives, liberation from samsara and enlightenment. For that purpose you are "giving away" your body, enjoyments and all your merits of the three times—past, present and future. That doesn't mean you are going to throw them in the garbage! It means you are completely offering everything to sentient beings from your heart without any attachment, miserliness or even the slightest feeling of sadness or loss. You give everything with a completely happy mind, just as you would give to the friend closest to your heart or to the person who has been kindest to you in your life, like your parents, who dedicated their lives to take care of you for so many years since your consciousness was conceived in your mother's womb.

It says here that you are going to give like that to "all" sentient beings. It doesn't say "except for my enemy and those people I don't like—who I hate even to see or remember." It says "all."

When you recite this verse, it is excellent to do the meditation on taking and giving (*tong-len*) so that it is not just left as words. That is a most amazing practice. In *tong-len* there is *tong-wa* "giving" and *len-pa* "taking." Here it doesn't actually talk about "taking," it just mentions "giving;" but if you wish you can first do the practice of taking and then do the giving.

The "taking" is taking on the suffering and causes of suffering of numberless sentient beings, along with the suffering of the places where they live. For example, in the hell realms there is the suffering of the burning iron ground, the weapons, the unbelievably huge cauldrons, the extremely hot molten hard-iron,[76] the iron burning houses with no doors or windows, and the ice mountains. Once beings are born in the hell realms they suffer for many billions, zillions and trillions of years—a most unbelievable amount of time—until the karma finishes. Then

76. See note 48.

another karma ripens and that has to be experienced for many billions and billions, zillions and zillions of eons until it finishes; and so it goes on. So take into your heart not only the suffering and their causes but also these terrifying places. Think that they melt into smoke, pollution or whatever form is most effective to destroy your ego and absorb to your heart, destroying your self-cherishing thought.

Each time you take on the suffering and causes of suffering from the numberless hell beings, think they achieve the state of dharmakaya, which is beyond suffering. Do the same for the hungry ghosts, animals, humans, suras, asuras and intermediate state beings. When you do this from the heart many eons of negative karma get purified.

When you give, start by giving all your numberless past, present and future merits. Then give all the resultant happiness that comes from these merits all the way up to enlightenment. After that, give your body in the form of a wish-granting jewel. Then give all your enjoyments, material possessions, the people around you, friends, family, even your children, father, mother, brothers and sisters—everything. Make charity of whatever you have to all sentient beings just as the Buddha did.

My root guru His Holiness Trijang Rinpoche used to say that you cannot give your body to sentient beings in its ordinary form. You should visualize it as a wish-granting jewel and offer it like that, thinking they receive everything they want from it. This is different from chöd practice. In chöd, there is the white distribution and the red distribution. In the red distribution your body becomes mountains of flesh, blood and bones and you make charity of that to the spirits. However, in the taking and giving practice, His Holiness Trijang Rinpoche advised to visualize your body as a wish-granting jewel. I think the idea is that sentient beings can receive everything they want from a wish-granting jewel. Visualize not just one small jewel but the whole sky filled with your body transformed into numberless wish-granting jewels as huge as mountains. Think you are giving to every sentient being whatever they need.

First, give everything to the numberless hell beings; think they received it and they own it. Then give to the numberless hungry ghosts; to the numberless animals and insects; to every human being; every sura; every asura; every intermediate state being; every arhat and every bodhisattva who is free from samsara. Normally we only talk about the six realms, but here we can offer to the arhats and bodhisattvas who are free from samsara, thinking that it helps them to complete the path and become enlightened.

Offer everything to each one of the numberless sentient beings; think they received it and that they own it. It is very good to think that it belongs to them—not that you have given it away but it is still yours. Thinking it belongs to them cuts the self-cherishing thought and the selfish mind.

Next, think that by receiving all these things the sentient beings achieve a pure land where there is no suffering—pure means no suffering—and where they can attain enlightenment. Numberless hell beings achieve a pure land where there is no suffering and only beauty. It is filled with wish-granting trees and whatever they wish for happens. Then numberless hungry ghosts, animals, human beings, suras, asuras and intermediate state beings also all achieve a pure land. You can also elaborate and think that they all receive a perfect human body, meet the Mahayana teachings and find a perfectly qualified guru who can reveal the path to enlightenment.

The conclusion is that by offering all of this to the numberless hell beings, hungry ghosts, animals, human beings, suras, asuras and intermediate state beings, they all actualize the complete path to enlightenment in their hearts and are liberated from the oceans of samsaric suffering along with all gross and subtle defilements. Then every hell being, hungry ghost, animal, human being, sura, asura and intermediate state being becomes enlightened in the form of the deity you are practicing. Rejoice that you have brought them all to the state of enlightenment.

This taking and giving meditation is a most amazing practice. It is the quick way to achieve enlightenment. Even just by doing this meditation once, you become rich in merits and make yourself the most fortunate, lucky person. When you take on the numberless hell beings' sufferings along with the causes of those sufferings, you collect numberless causes of enlightenment, numberless merits. It is the same when you take on the sufferings of the numberless hungry ghosts, animals, human beings, suras, asuras and intermediate state beings. When you do this practice, you collect seven times numberless merits, or numberless causes of enlightenment. Can you imagine?

Then each time you give your body as a wish-granting jewel to numberless hell beings, you collect numberless causes for enlightenment. It is the same when you offer your possessions and your merits. You have so many belongings and by using them to make charity to the numberless sentient beings, you can collect numberless merits—the causes of enlightenment—with each one. Practicing this way causes the greatest success, enlightenment. By the way, it also causes liberation from samsara, the happiness of future lives and the happiness of this life.

I'm saying what *can* be done as you recite this verse, how to expand the practice and give everything. But if you can't do all of this, at least do the meditation on giving, so that it is not just reciting words.

Death

By giving away all, I will be liberated from the oceans
    of samsaric suffering
And my mind will achieve the sorrowless state.

Since I have to leave everything (at death)
It is best to (now) give it away to every single
    sentient being.

Here, the sorrowless state refers to liberation from all the oceans of samsaric suffering; and not only that, but also to the great liberation of enlightenment. The verse is saying that sooner or later you will die and at that time you have to leave behind everything: your material possessions, family, friends and even this body that you cherish more than numberless other sentient beings or any other precious thing. Even if you are a king with a great entourage, the president of a country populated by millions or just very wealthy with a jeweled palace made of diamonds and gold, you cannot stay forever. No matter how large your family or how great your wealth, no matter how powerful your army or how many bodyguards you have, no matter how beautiful the place or country where you live, you will have to leave everything behind. Only the bare consciousness goes to the next life. It is like pulling a hair from butter; the hair is extracted and the butter left behind. Therefore, since anyway you will have to give all these things away, it is best to now give everything to every single sentient being.

Bodhicitta means wanting to be used by others

Having given this body to sentient beings[77]
To use *however* they want that makes them happy,

---

77. Rinpoche's comment: "The term used here for sentient beings is *lu-chen*— 'physical beings.' *lu* is body, *chen* means having, so *lu-chen* refers to all sentient beings or to 'those having a physical body.' Probably it means 'those who take birth under the control of delusion and karma,' but I'm not sure why it is used here, because not every sentient being has a body. Formless beings don't have a body and intermediate state beings don't have a gross body. There might be a reason, but I haven't seen it yet."

Whether they always kill me, criticize, beat me or
   whatever,
It is totally up to them.

This is saying, "I have given this body to be used by sentient beings in whatever way makes them most happy." This is very, very important. You must have this thought to practice or to actualize bodhicitta. I often hear people say, "Oh, these people are just *using* me!" Even sometimes at meetings in our centers I hear this. That is because they are not practicing bodhicitta. One time I wrote a letter to a center saying, "Bodhisattvas *want* to be used by sentient beings." That is what the bodhisattvas' attitude is. They actually accept it. The worldly mind thinks that being used by others is bad, the worst thing, but bodhisattvas are most happy to accept this. If you want to achieve enlightenment, you have to practice bodhicitta, and this is exactly what the bodhisattvas' attitude is. Their happiest practice is to be used by sentient beings. It is what they are always looking for.

I heard that Kadampa Geshe Potowa was always happy to find an opportunity to serve others. These are not ordinary beings; they have actualized bodhicitta, the three principal aspects of the path to enlightenment, tantric realizations, all of that. Whenever other people asked Kadampa Geshe Potowa to do a puja for them, he was unbelievably happy to do so.

Our motivation should always be to be used by others for their happiness. If you are going to practice bodhicitta, this is what you have to accept. If what you want is to liberate sentient beings from the oceans of samsaric suffering and enlighten them, you need to achieve enlightenment. If you want to achieve enlightenment, you need to practice bodhicitta. The bodhisattvas' attitude is to always totally dedicate their lives day and night to be used by other sentient beings for their happiness. This is what they are seeking and wishing for all the time. You have to know that. If you feel like that, there is the opportunity to gradually become closer and closer to bodhicitta and have the realization. If you are able to change your mind into an attitude wishing to be used by others for their happiness, this is exactly what the bodhisattva attitude is.

Anyway, it says here, "I have given this body to be used *however* they want for their happiness." This is an incredible complete and total change of mind. It is very important to remember this— especially when somebody slaps you! When we do the *Guru Puja* every *tsog* day there is the practice of taking and giving:[78]

> And thus, perfect pure compassionate gurus,
> I seek your blessings that all negativities, obscurations
>   and sufferings of mother migrators
> May without exception ripen upon me right now,
> And that by giving my happiness and virtue to others
> All migrators may experience happiness.

If you have been doing the meditation at that time, then you have already given everything away. If you left out the meditation and just recited the prayer without thinking of the meaning, of course there is nothing. But if you have been doing the meditation, then you have already given your body, your merits and everything to every sentient being many times. Therefore, it makes no sense to get upset when somebody gets angry at you or scolds you. It would be a very good examination if while you were chanting so beautifully about giving everything to sentient beings, somebody who was good at it came along and slapped you!

Once when Kyabje Khunu Lama Rinpoche was giving His Holiness the Dalai Lama an extensive commentary on Shantideva's *Guide* in Bodhgaya, he told him this story. There was a man sitting meditating outside Tashi Lhunpo Monastery. A person passing by asked him, "What are you doing?" and he replied,

---

78. V. 95. This verse is not Rinpoche's translation; it comes from the *FPMT Retreat Prayer Book*.

"I'm practicing patience." Then that person said to the man practicing patience, "Eat kaka!" and he immediately retorted, "Eat it yourself!" His Holiness has told this story many times.

If you remember the taking and giving practice when somebody slaps you—wow! If you remember all the benefits that you receive from sentient beings—all the numberless past lives' happiness, all the present life's happiness, then liberation and enlightenment—it is most unimaginable. Even if you just think of enlightenment. Wow! There is no way to get angry back. There is no way you would take people to court. You only want to respect others and give them happiness in return. Since you have already given your body to be used by sentient beings in whatever way makes them most happy, when you see that they have found your body useful, it is unbelievable, most amazing, the happiest thing.

This is the reality, but if you listen to the advice of mundane worldly people who do not practice Dharma, then of course it will be different. If you listen to Western culture, which is based on anger and attachment, the advice will be totally opposite to the Dharma and totally opposite to bodhicitta. This point is very important.

> Even if they play with my body,
> Ridicule me, put me down or make fun of me,
> Whatever they do, since I have given this body to them,
> What is the point of retaliating?

This kind of attitude is totally completely opposite to the way people in the world live their lives. Worldly people think that if somebody harms you, you should harm them back immediately, even twice as much. If a person slaps you once, you should slap them back twice, ten times, even one hundred times in return. This is how they think; their attitude and behavior are totally opposite to bodhicitta.

Always meaningful for others

Let this body only do actions that cause no harm
   to others,
And whoever looks at or thinks of me,
May it never be meaningless for them.

This prayer is very important. You are praying to become wish-fulfilling for anyone who looks at or thinks of you, not only other people but even animals, insects and spirits. Just by seeing you, remembering you, hearing your voice, touching you, or whatever, may all their mental and physical sicknesses be healed, may they find faith and devotion in Buddha, Dharma and Sangha and may they develop compassion, bodhicitta and the good heart, actualize the tantric path and achieve enlightenment.

Whoever focuses on me—
Whether with anger or devotion—
May that always be the cause for them
To achieve every success.

May all who say unpleasant things,
Harm, mock or make fun of me
Have the fortune to achieve enlightenment.

This is the bodhisattva attitude. Even if people get angry at you, make fun of you, criticize, beat or harm you, in return you pray for that only to become meaningful for them and the cause of whatever happiness and success they seek. It is most wonderful to pray like this. It would be very nice if somebody famous could make this into a song for young people to be drawn to and sing. Even just hearing the words and taking these ideas into their lives, would give them more methods, more psychology. All of this is the best and deepest psychology. It does not harm sentient beings, but only benefits and brings happiness to them, and sooner or later the result will be enlightenment.

No matter how others behave toward you, whether they think badly of you or harm you, in return you should pray to become wish-fulfilling for every sentient being, not only human beings but even animals and so on.

> May I become a guide for those who are guideless,
> A leader for those who are entering the path,
> A ship, a boat and a bridge
> For all who wish to cross (over water).

There are so many sentient beings, even amongst humans, who are guideless. They are guideless in Dharma and guideless even in worldly activities for the happiness of this life. Pray to become a guide for these numberless beings who need help.

> May I become a beautiful garden for those who seek one,
> A light for those who look for light,
> Bedding for those who wish to rest
> And a servant for all who want me as their servant.

Here, the word used for light is *mar-me,* which means "butter lamp." *Mar* is butter and *me* is lamp, but it is referring to any kind of light. The idea is to become a light for anybody who needs one. Bedding includes a bed, blankets, pillows, everything. In the West there are big beds that you can roll around in and sleep anywhere.

There is no mention of being a toilet. Of course, it would be many thousands of pages if everything was mentioned, so I think Shantideva abbreviated. But if you want, you can pray to be a bathroom for those who need one. Especially when you go to Tibet, most of the time there is no toilet and you have to go outside to the "free bathroom." Anyway, here we are training our minds in the bodhisattva attitude. Therefore, even if it is not mentioned here, you can pray to become absolutely anything that sentient beings need.

Then pray to become a servant for those who need one. That is a fantastic, most wonderful prayer. It is another total and complete change of attitude. Usually the ego wants other sentient beings to become its servant. You can use others who are numberless, but others can't use you, who is just one. That is the self-cherishing mind's dictatorship. It has no meaning and makes no sense. But when your mind thinks in this way—wanting to be used by others—you have such an incredibly joyful life. You have the happiest life. There is no unhappiness or depression. You are always so unbelievably happy to be used by others. You feel fortunate to be used by others. Can you imagine what it is like when your attitude has totally changed like that?

The means of living and the cause of happiness for numberless sentient beings

When there is no time to go through all the verses, just do these last three that cover everything. They are really very wonderful. Use them as a motivation in the morning and at other times. Remember them as you go through the day. It would also be good to chant them.

> Like a wish-granting jewel,
> A wish-fulfilling vase, powerful mantra,
> Great medicine and a wish-granting tree,
> May I fulfill all the wishes of sentient beings.

Here you are praying to be the "cause of happiness" for sentient beings.[79] How? Various examples are given, starting with a wish-granting jewel.

79. See the next verse "May I always be the means of living and the cause of happiness for sentient beings equaling the limitless sky."

If you have the merit to find a wish-granting jewel in the ocean, you clean it in three different ways, put it on top of a banner on the fifteenth day of the Tibetan lunar month—that night is usually full moon—and put the banner on the roof of your house. Then whatever external enjoyment or material thing that you need, you just have to pray for it and it immediately materializes due to your good karma, merits and the condition of the power of that wish-granting jewel.

The wish-granting jewel is given as an example because it is the most valuable of external precious materials, but of course it can only give material comfort; it can't give realizations or a good rebirth, and it can't give liberation from samsara or enlightenment. Therefore, when you pray to become like a wish-granting jewel for sentient beings, don't think only of giving them material things. Pray to be able to purify their negative karma, cause them to get a higher rebirth and stop reincarnating in the lower realms, and guide them to liberation from samsara and enlightenment.

Then pray to become like a "wish-fulfilling vase" for other sentient beings, so they immediately receive whatever happiness they think of, and to be like a "powerful mantra." When somebody has chanted many hundreds of thousands or millions of mantras, they can succeed in everything they need to do to benefit others, whether it is healing sicknesses, controlling the weather, pacifying, increasing, controlling or wrathful actions. Therefore, pray to become like this for sentient beings.

"Great medicine" might be *arura*. There is ordinary arura, which is one of the three fundamental medicines; the Tibetan Medical Centre uses this to make medicine. Then there is real arura, which is extremely rare and can cure all sicknesses. That is what Medicine Buddha is holding. There is said to be real arura offered inside the heart of the Maitreya Buddha at Tashi Lhunpo Monastery in Tibet as a relic. The statue is about four stories high and I heard that if you stand at the second level against the heart all your sicknesses are cured. Some medicines used to contain real arura. His Holiness Trijang Rinpoche had a medicine from Tibet containing real arura that had incredible healing powers when worn. Pray to become healing for sentient beings like this great medicine.

Then pray to become like "a wish-granting tree." In the pure lands there are wish-granting trees and whatever you pray for is actualized immediately. It is great to pray to become like this for sentient beings.

In this text, which comes at the end of the chöd practice composed by the great lama Kachen Yeshe Gyaltsen, the last line of this verse is "May I become wish-fulfilling for sentient beings." In Shantideva's *Guide to the Bodhisattva's Way of Life,* the last line is different.[80]

When you need to abbreviate the verses even more, you can just read these last two verses. Even that much is very good.

> Just like the sky and the great elements
> Earth, (water, fire and wind),
> May I always be the means of living and the cause of
>   happiness
> For sentient beings equaling the limitless sky.

Here you are praying to become the means of living in so many different ways for the unimaginable number of sentient beings, like the earth and the other great elements.

The earth is used by sentient beings to make roads, build factories and houses to live in, as fields to grow crops in, and in so many unbelievable ways for their happiness. Pray to be used exactly like that by sentient beings. This is an unbelievable prayer. Water is used for drinking, washing, sailing and for pleasure in so many different ways by sentient beings for their happiness. Pray to be beneficial and used exactly like that by others. Fire is

---

80. Stephen Batchelor and Alan Wallace translate this verse (*Guide*, ch. 3 v. 19/20) with the additional prayer to become like a wish-granting cow.

used by sentient beings to cook, keep warm, heat cold places and so on. Pray to be used exactly like fire in so many different ways by sentient beings. Then pray to be used exactly like the wind, which sentient beings use for breathing or air conditioning; and like the sky, which they use for travelling and movement. Pray to be beneficial and to be used by sentient beings however they wish for their happiness, just like these great elements.

It says here, "May I always be the means of living and the cause of happiness" for others. That means not only when your mind is OK and you are in a good mood, but all the time, even when you are in a bad mood or depressed. You are praying to be used like this always and forever.

This bodhisattva attitude makes your life so beneficial and meaningful for sentient beings. You are praying to be used by others for their happiness however they want. The point is that this practice of bodhicitta is totally against the ego. It is totally opposite to the self-cherishing thought. It diminishes the self-cherishing thought and the selfish mind that hinder your achievement of enlightenment, liberation from samsara, the happiness of future lives and even the happiness of this life. The selfish mind harms you and harms all sentient beings from life to life, and this bodhisattva attitude totally eliminates that.

At the end, I think it is very good to recite the prayer that His Holiness the Dalai Lama always explains when giving the bodhisattva wishing vows. It is not in this text but it is also from *A Guide to the Bodhisattva's Way of Life.*[81]

> As long as space exists,
> As long as sentient beings exist,
> May I too abide and eliminate the suffering of
>   sentient beings.

81. Ch. 10, v. 55.

The bodhisattva attitude

By dedicating your life to others in this way, you can enjoy every day. There is always deep happiness in your heart instead of jealousy and so many other sufferings. When you follow your ego, negative emotional thoughts and self-cherishing, even though nobody else tortures you, you are constantly tortured by attachment, anger and so on. You create so many problems and so much negative karma and then you suffer. You harm others and yourself and then you have to experience the result by again having so many problems. Your whole life goes by like this until one day death comes and that's it; your life finishes in suffering.

With this bodhisattva attitude, you can enjoy life, because you experience it with Dharma by letting go of delusion, ego and especially the self-cherishing thought. You can live with inner peace and happiness, in deep joy and satisfaction by practicing Dharma. Then your heart is opened all the time day and night. You are able to help other sentient beings and yourself. All your activities are accomplished and you achieve enlightenment, ceasing all gross and subtle delusions and completing all the qualities of realization. You are able to liberate others from suffering and delusion and bring them to enlightenment.

If you can live your life in this way, with this total change of mind to the bodhisattva attitude, you will have deep happiness all the time. There will be no regrets now and no regrets in the future, just greater and greater happiness up to enlightenment. You will be able to help both yourself and others.

In the West, millions of people suffer from depression, but if you dedicate your life in the morning to numberless sentient beings, you will have unbelievable joy and happiness the whole day. Cherishing the I opens the door to all suffering, while cherishing others opens the door to all happiness. When you live your life every day for others, the door to depression, relationship problems and all such things is closed and instead there is incredible joy and excitement.

With the bodhisattva attitude you become wish-fulfilling for others. All sentient beings have been wish-fulfilling and kind to you since beginningless rebirths and now you become wish-fulfilling for them. From this, all your wishes for happiness will be fulfilled, even your wish to achieve liberation and enlightenment and to benefit others by causing them to have happiness in this and future lives, liberation and enlightenment. You will become the cause of all this for others. This is how to overcome all problems.

Recite this motivation in the morning and then during the day, if somebody gets angry with you, scolds or abuses you or says nasty words, whatever happens, remember this motivation. If you ask somebody for help and they refuse, remember this motivation. Then, instead of generating anger, delusions and all that junk and garbage, you will have great peace and happiness. The point is to generate this motivation in the morning and then remember it throughout the day, especially when something happens and there is the danger of harmful thoughts of anger, attachment and so forth arising. By remembering this motivation and keeping your mind in it, you will free yourself from creating negative karma. There will be so much peace and happiness in your life now, and in future the result will be enlightenment for you and for all sentient beings.

Light of the Path

6. Four Wrong Concepts[82]

A Motivation for taking the Eight Mahayana Precepts

Today I thought to read a motivation that His Holiness the Dalai Lama taught one time when giving the eight Mahayana precepts in Dharamsala. His Holiness gave the precepts quite a number of times. Once when I was staying in Dharamsala for a few months, His Holiness requested his senior tutor, His Holiness Ling Rinpoche, to give the eight Mahayana precepts in the temple. Inside and outside the temple was filled with monks and lay people and His Holiness took the precepts along with everybody else. His Holiness Ling Rinpoche gave a motivation as well as the definition of each of the four major and four secondary vows.[83]

Another time His Holiness gave the precepts, not inside but outside the temple. The motivation was very effective so I got the tape and wrote it down. After listening to that motivation, my mind kind of changed and I could think of others. I think it was just a blessing, not the actual realization, and of course it didn't last long because I didn't put effort into it, even though I planned to do so.

---

82. This commentary is based on *Light of the Path*, 11 September (morning and evening) 2009.
83. For teachings on the eight Mahayana precepts and the actual ceremony, see *The Direct and Unmistaken Method* and *Teachings from the Vajrasattva Retreat*.

Motivation: the four wrong concepts[84]

Think:

> I and all sentient beings have been suffering in samsara
> from beginningless rebirths up to now because of these
> four wrong concepts:[85]
>
>> While the aggregates are not I, the self,
>> Because of looking at the aggregates as the self
>>   and being attached,
>> I and all sentient beings have been born and
>>   suffered in samsara
>> Numberless times from beginningless rebirths
>>   up to now.
>>
>> While samsaric pleasure is only suffering,
>> Because of looking at samsaric pleasure as real
>>   happiness and being attached,
>> I and all sentient beings have been born and
>>   suffered in samsara
>> Numberless times from beginningless rebirths
>>   up to now.
>>
>> While this body is dirty,
>> Because of looking at the body as completely
>>   clean and being attached,

---

84. I have not seen a copy of the original motivation by His Holiness transcribed by Rinpoche and Rinpoche does not seem to have read this out. Therefore I extracted and summarized the following motivation from Rinpoche's teaching and it is not part of the original discourse.

85. *Steps on the Path to Enlightenment, Volume 1*, p. 312, lists these four wrong concepts as: "Perceiving impermanent things to be permanent, suffering as pleasure, the impure as pure and the selfless as having an independent absolute reality." That is the order in which they are given in Lama Tsongkhapa's *Great Treatise*.

> I and all sentient beings have been born and
>   suffered in samsara
> Numberless times from beginningless rebirths
>   up to now.

> While all compounded phenomena are in the
>   nature of impermanence,
> Because of looking at compounded phenomena
>   as permanent and being attached,
> I and all sentient beings have been born in sam-
>   sara and suffered
> Numberless times from beginningless rebirths
>   up to now.

If I continue to follow these four wrong concepts, I will experience unimaginable sufferings endlessly. Just being free from the ocean of samsaric sufferings and its causes is not enough:

> All sufferings, obstacles, misfortunes and unde-
> sirable things come from cherishing the I.

Therefore, the I is something to let go of.

> All happiness—my past happiness from begin-
> ningless rebirths, present happiness, future hap-
> piness, liberation and enlightenment—comes
> from bodhicitta, the good heart cherishing and
> wanting to benefit others.

Therefore, other sentient beings are unbelievably precious, kind and dear. To cause the numberless sentient beings to have the happiness of this life, future lives, liberation from samsara and enlightenment, I myself must achieve enlightenment; therefore I am going to take the eight Mahayana precepts.

ONE: LOOKING AT THE AGGREGATES
AS BEING THE SELF

While the aggregates are not I, the self,
Because of looking at the aggregates as the self and being
attached,
I and all sentient beings have been born and suffered in
samsara
Numberless times from beginningless rebirths up to now.

There is no I or self inside this body. The body is not the self, nor is the mind. To elaborate by going through each of the five aggregates: form is not I, feeling is not I, cognition is not I, the compounding aggregates[86] are not I, and consciousness is not I. None of these five aggregates is the I or the self and even all together they are not the self. The aggregates themselves are not I, nor can I be found *on* the aggregates. Nowhere from the tips of your hair down to your toes can you can find the I, the self. (The "I," or "self," are the same thing.)

What can't be found are two things. First, the real I that you believe right now is sitting on a cushion taking the eight Maha-yana precepts: "*I* am here in a hall in North Carolina taking the eight Mahayana precepts." That is the "real" I and it can't be found. "Real" means "*not* merely labeled by the mind," which means it is "existing from its own side." When ordinary people call something "real," they are actually talking about the object to be refuted (Tib: *gag-cha*). The object to be refuted is something

---

86. Rinpoche's comment: "Compounding aggregates in Tibetan is *du-je kyi phung-po*—the word is the title. There are fifty-one mental factors and when you take out two—feeling and cognition—forty-nine are left. Those forty-nine mental factors are called *du-je kyi phung-po* ('*du byed kyi phung po*), 'compounding aggregates,' because they 'compound' the result. The Tibetan is similar to *du-je* ('*dus byas*), which means 'causative' or 'compound-ed' phenomena, i.e. the action has been done. But this is 'compound-ing' phenomena, because it is compound-*ing* or produc-*ing* its result. The translation needs to be made precise."

that appears to the hallucinated mind to "exist from its own side" and is held by ignorance as one hundred percent true, but in reality it is not there. In everyday life, when people use the common word "real," what they are referring to is actually the object to be refuted.

Therefore, this real I that you believe is taking the precepts and the real I that I believe is giving them is not there. Well, I can't say that everybody in the hall is thinking that way! But anyway, in reality it is not there. There is no such real I giving the eight Mahayana precepts and no such real I taking them. It can't be found. Nowhere from the tips of your hair down to your toes can that be found.

Second, not only can that real I not be found, but you can't even find the merely imputed I that does exist. Even that can't be found. You can find it in the United States and right now you can find it in this hall but you can't find it on these aggregates. If you look for the merely labeled I, you can't find it.

Which I is to be refuted?

So there is a question: When you look for the I and can't find it, is that the definition of realizing emptiness? My view is that that needs to be checked.

The text[87] mentions three I's: The merely labeled I; the real I that is not merely labeled by the mind but existing from its own side; and the general I, the I that is not specifically merely labeled or truly existent, it is just I.

These three are basically different ways an individual can view the I. By looking at the I as merely labeled, we can specify that there is a "merely labeled I"—which actually accords with reality—then apply the label "merely labeled I" and look for it.

---

87. It is not clear which text Rinpoche is referring to here, but the "three I's" are mentioned in Lama Tsongkhapa's *Middle-Length Exposition of the Stages of the Path*. See *Tsongkhapa's Final Exposition of Wisdom*, p. 57.

Then we can specify that there is a "real I" or "truly existent I"—
the I we believe is inside this body and we feel to be something
very truly existent from its own side—then apply the label "truly
existent I" and look for it.[88] Then when you are not thinking of
the I as being either truly existent or merely labeled but just I, that
is the general I. For example, you can look for the truly existent
book, the merely labeled book, or just the general book without
either of those being specified.

So when we look for the I and can't find it, which I are we
talking about? That needs to be checked because neither the truly
existent I nor the merely labeled I can be found, but if you look
for the merely labeled I or the general I on these aggregates and
can't find them, *that* becomes falling into nihilism.[89]

In the lam-rim it is explained that if you look for the vase—not
the "truly existent" or "real" vase that is the object to be refuted,
but just "the vase"—at the end of the analysis when you can't
find the vase anywhere, it is not clear what the vase is, because
you didn't touch the object to be refuted. Then you fall into
nihilism or destroy dependent arising.

The first of the four vital points of analysis is "understanding
the object to be refuted."[90] The reason that comes first is because
it makes no sense to look for the merely labeled I or general I and
not find it. Recently I checked and saw a few paragraphs in different places talking about this mistaken way of analyzing. This
is analysis, but it is done in the wrong way because the object to
be refuted is missed out. Because the object to be refuted is not

88. Rinpoche's comment: "The Vaibhashika, Sautrantika and Cittamatra schools
all believe there is a truly existent I. The Svatantrika and Prasangika schools—
although they have a different understanding of what 'truly existent' means—do
not believe this exists."

89. This is because—as Rinpoche goes on to explain—the merely labeled I does
exist as a dependent arising and is therefore not the object to be refuted; whereas
the truly existent I does not exist at all and is a mental fabrication. Therefore, it
is the truly existent I that we need to realize is empty and this realization will not
destroy the view of dependent arising.

90. Analyzing by way of the four vital points is one of the main techniques for
meditating on emptiness. Pabongka Rinpoche explains that it is particularly suitable for beginners, see *Liberation, Part Three*, pp. 274–90.

touched, the result is unclear and you can't point out what the vase is. You cannot come to the conclusion that the vase exists as a dependent arising, which is its conventional truth, or the "truth for the all-obscuring mind."[91]

Analyzing this way doesn't support dependent arising but only destroys it, therefore you are lost! This kind of analysis is not meditating on emptiness. Meditating on emptiness should harm ignorance, but this doesn't harm ignorance; ignorance is left there. Therefore, we need to be very specific about exactly which I it is that, when we look for it and can't find it, means we are seeing emptiness. Anyway, this is just a tiny drop to give you some idea.

The realization of emptiness

Therefore, the real I that is now taking the eight Mahayana precepts and the real I that is now giving them are not there. That real I can't be found *in* this body or *on* these aggregates. It is totally empty. It has *total* non-existence from its own side. It is *totally* non-existent right there from where it is appearing to your hallucinated mind.

Normally I say that this is my mudra for meditating on emptiness. The mudra for the object to be refuted is to [bring your hands toward yourself palms facing upwards] expressing that the real I appears to exist from there, from its own side. Then the mudra for seeing emptiness is [to turn your palms downwards and move the hands down away from yourself] showing that the real I is *totally* non-existent, right there from where it is appearing. It is totally non-existent right there.

As sentient beings, everything appears to us to be truly existent.

91. *Kün-dzob den-pa* is usually translated as "conventional" truth and *don-dam den-pa* as "ultimate" truth. Rinpoche translates *kün-dzob den-pa* as "truth for the all-obscuring mind" to bring out the full meaning that although conventional truth is true for a valid conventional consciousness, it obscures the ultimate nature of reality (emptiness).

Only in meditative equipoise with the wisdom directly perceiving emptiness is there no truly existent appearance and no hallucination. Otherwise, even when arising from that concentration, hallucination is there again. The truly existent view ceases only when the subtle defilement of ignorance—the negative imprint that projects the truly existent view—is ceased and there is no more concept of true existence. Buddha doesn't have dualistic view, the truly existent view, but we sentient beings do and that is why for us there is always the appearance of a truly existent I. The I appears to us to be truly existent and because of not having realized emptiness, we hold to its existing that way.

After realizing that the I is empty, there is no longer the concept holding it to be truly existent. The simultaneously born concept of true existence is still there—that remains right up to the eighth ground—but not the clinging to true existence. The difference between the way of apprehending an object before realizing emptiness and after realizing it is like the difference between the sky and the earth. Before realizing emptiness, there is a strong holding on to true existence. A person who hasn't realized emptiness apprehends the I to be truly existent and clings strongly to that. But after realizing the I to be empty, that total holding on to the I as truly existent is no longer there.

It is like looking back after crossing over the sand and seeing a mirage. The sunlight hitting the sand creates a vision of water and it really looks like there is water. But because you just came from there, you have the understanding that there is no water there. There is an appearance of water *but* at the same time you have the realization that there is no water. There is no clinging or total holding on to there being water.

The evolution of samsara and the suffering of the six realms

This I is *totally* empty. It is *totally* non-existent. Not only now, not only from last night, not only from birth, but from beginningless time. It has been empty and non-existent from the beginning. It never came into existence. But while it is like this, we have the hallucination that it exists from its own side.

The I that is just this second merely imputed by the mind, the very next second appears back to the hallucinated mind as not merely labeled. That appearance is a mental fabrication, but we let the mind hold onto it as one hundred percent true and in that moment, we create the root of samsara, ignorance.

This happens because we have been following ignorance and have been under the control of ignorance from beginningless rebirths. Ignorance has been our guru and we have been listening to everything it says with total trust up to now. Because of that, all the other negative emotional thoughts and wrong concepts arise: anger, attachment and ignorance along with the many different branches and types of these three poisonous minds. It is said that 84,000 teachings were given by the Buddha because, when elaborated, there are 84,000 different types of delusion.

Ignorance motivates karma, which plants a karmic seed on the mere I. This is according to the Prasangika school, but how can an imprint be left without the continuum of the mind?[92] From that seed, rebirth is produced. It is because of this ignorance—the self-grasping of the person and self-grasping of the aggregates—that we have been suffering in samsara from beginningless rebirths up to now.

Numberless times we have been born in each of the hell realms—the eight major cold hells, the eight major hot hells and the neighboring hells—from beginningless rebirths.

Numberless times we have been born in the hungry ghost realm. Hungry ghosts experience the heaviest suffering of hunger and thirst for hundreds, thousands and even tens of thousands of years. They cannot find even one drop of water, not even

92. Here we are being challenged to understand the meaning of the Prasangika school view that imprints are left on the mere I.

dampness on the ground or even a spoonful of food for hundreds of thousands of years. It is the most unbearable suffering and we have been born in that realm and experienced it numberless times from beginningless rebirths.

Numberless times we have been born as animals and experienced the suffering of being extremely foolish and ignorant, as well as the unbelievably, unbelievably heavy suffering of being eaten alive. Wherever an animal is, its enemy is right there. Whether it is in the water, in the forest or underground, due to karma, wherever the animal is, its enemy is always nearby and it can be eaten any time.

In recent years I have been telling people that some time ago, when I was in an airplane, the thought came to me that when you look down at the ocean it seems very peaceful and calm, but when you think about the creatures that live in the water—wow, what suffering! What unimaginable suffering! There are big ones the size of a mountain that eat an unbelievable number of small ones. They eat whatever comes next to their mouth. Then there are many small ones who feed off the bodies of the big ones.

Animals are constantly running in fear of being eaten. While they are escaping from their enemies, they're looking for other animals to eat at the same time. It is just amazing; an unbelievable state of fear. Look at the birds. When a bird lands on the ground to eat food, it looks this way and that in every direction. You have to understand *why*—there is always fear. Wherever an animal is, its enemy comes. There is one creature I have seen that lives underground. It digs a tunnel in the earth but then snakes crawl in to eat it. Sometimes it will come out and make a lot of noise until the snake goes away. At the moment, we are not living with the constant fear of being eaten alive as we run to eat another creature alive. Many human beings in this world do eat creatures alive, but due to having met the Buddhadharma and due to Buddha's kindness and compassion, we are not doing that.

It is just amazing that we have not been born as those animals. Wow! It is just amazing that we have such unbelievable comfort and pleasure, especially the freedom and opportunity to practice Dharma. Like today, for example, right now taking the eight Mahayana precepts and doing retreat with lam-rim meditation and tantric practice, the quickest path to enlightenment. On the foundation of lam-rim we do the *Guru Puja,* which is the quickest way to achieve enlightenment. It has so many methods to purify obstacles and collect extensive merits, the necessary conditions. It is just amazing. We do not realize enough the situation those animals are in, all their continuous suffering and fear. We are simply not aware. We have such unbelievable comfort and pleasure that we can't imagine it. We are totally spoiled and pampered—yet we are still unable to practice Dharma.

We have been born as all those different creatures living in the ocean numberless times. We have been born as whales the size of mountains and as tiny creatures that can only be seen through a microscope. We have been born as jellyfish and have been eaten numberless times. We have continuously suffered all of this numberless times from beginningless rebirths.

Even the animals that live with human beings have unbelievable suffering. They suffer from heat and cold, from being tortured, made to carry heavy loads and pull carriages. I see many beasts in India with their noses running and breathing "haaah haaah" because the load they are pulling is too heavy. Horses and cows are used as long as they can produce milk or be ridden, then killed for meat when they are old and no longer able to walk or be useful. Usually horse meat is not eaten but in Mongolia and some other countries it is very common to eat horse meat and drink horse's milk.

These animals cannot say anything. They have no freedom. They cannot express their feelings or say how much they are suffering. Can you imagine the difference between us as human beings and them? Wow! We don't have the kind of problems they face for even a day. Therefore, if we make no use of this incredible life we have now with all its comfort, wealth and so on to practice Dharma and instead waste it—there is no greater loss. I am not going to go through all the quotations in *A Guide to the Bodhisattva's Way of Life,* but Shantideva says:[93]

> If I don't collect merit
> While I have the fortune to enjoy virtue,
> What can I do when I am born totally ignorant
> And suffering in the lower realms?

If we don't practice Dharma, purify, collect merit and attain the path now while we have this incredible opportunity, what will we do when born in the lower realms due to negative karma collected from beginningless rebirths and which we have still not purified or finished experiencing? Nothing. There is nothing that can be done in the lower realms, except just suffer for eons and eons and eons until the karma finishes.

Numberless times we have been born as human beings and suffered. Humans have eight types of suffering. In the *Great Treatise,* these eight are each explained in five outlines.[94] There is the suffering of birth, old age, sickness, death, worry and fear about meeting what you don't want, not being able to find what you do want, not getting any satisfaction when you do find what you want and the suffering of the aggregates. The Rolling Stones' singer expressed our inability to find satisfaction exactly from his own experience. He was somebody who was world famous, had a good reputation, wealth, friends and everything else, but he could not get any satisfaction from all of this. Human beings have all these sufferings and the suffering of the aggregates.

Numberless times we have been born as suras and asuras and suffered. The mental suffering of the suras when they experience

93. Ch. 4, v. 18.
94. *Volume One,* pp. 272–79.

the five signs of nearing death is much heavier than the physical sufferings of the hell beings.

For example, sometimes I think that beggars who live on the street have not that much worry. Every day they beg for some food and live on that. They don't have to worry about having a bad reputation or not being richer or better than others like wealthy people with businesses. Millionaires, billionaires and zillionaires have all that wealth and huge mansions, but so much worry.

Recently I saw a very wealthy American man on TV showing off his house. He has a mansion built on the water by the side of a lake and he was showing off all the many rooms and beds and boats and comfort. The good thing about being wealthy is that even if you don't have the Dharma, you can help by doing good things for others with a sincere heart and compassion. Otherwise, there is nothing, just a lot of worry and fear about your business or reputation.

Wealthy people are always anxious and afraid that somebody else will become richer or more powerful and that they will lose their reputation or wealth. Even though they already have enough money for many, many lifetimes, still they have an unbelievable amount of anxiety. There are many problems at work, relationship problems at home and a lot of pressure and stress all the time. The beggar on the street doesn't have that much concern.

When Gelek Rinpoche was living in Delhi, he mentioned during teachings that the poor laborers working outside under the hot sun building roads or doing construction work look up through the windows of the large houses and see the air conditioning and fans. For them it seems like heaven and they think, "Those people have so much comfort and pleasure! How wonderful their lives are! They have no problems, only happiness!" At the same time, the wealthy people living in the houses look down at the laborers and think, "Those people working on the road have such a good, simple life with no heavy responsibilities or problems!" They are attracted to the poor people's lives because they have so many business and relationship problems and a lot of worry and fear.

In a similar way, Kyabje Chöden Rinpoche explained that the mental suffering of the devas is heavier than the physical suffering of animals.

Numberless times we have been born and suffered like this in samsara due to ignorance, looking at the aggregates as being the I, the self, when in reality there is no I or self. This is the main wrong concept and from that come three others.

Two: LOOKING AT SAMSARIC PLEASURE AS REAL HAPPINESS

As I have already explained:[95]

> While samsaric pleasure is only suffering,
> Because of looking at samsaric pleasure as real happiness
>   and being attached,
> I and all sentient beings have been born and suffered in
>   samsara
> Numberless times from beginningless rebirths up to now.

Samsaric pleasure is only suffering, but because of labeling it and looking at it as real happiness and then being attached, we have been continuously suffering in samsara from beginningless rebirths.

---

95. See *Give Up Stretching the Legs*, pp. 79–89.

THREE: LOOKING AT THE BODY AS CLEAN

While this body is dirty,
Because of looking at the body as completely clean and
  being attached,
I and all sentient beings have been born and suffered in
  samsara
Numberless times from beginningless rebirths up to now.

This body is like a garbage can or a septic tank that collects all the waste from the toilet. Can you imagine being inside a septic tank? That is what this body is like. Nagarjuna said the body is "a container of thirty-six dirty things."

Khunu Lama Rinpoche explained that before food is eaten, it is clean, but after going inside the body, it is dirty. Whether it comes out from the mouth, the ears or the holes in the lower part of the body, it is dirty. When food is put in a container or pot it doesn't become dirty, but when it is put inside the body it becomes dirty. The reason it is dirty is because the inside of the body is dirty. This shows that the nature of the body is dirty.

While this body is dirty because of looking at it as completely clean and being attached to it, we have been continuously taking rebirth and experiencing suffering in samsara from beginningless rebirths up to now.

FOUR: LOOKING AT IMPERMANENT PHENOMENA AS PERMANENT[96]

While all compounded phenomena are in the nature of
  impermanence,
Because of looking at compounded phenomena as
  permanent and being attached,

96. Meditation on impermanence is dealt with in *Cutting the Concept of Permanence*.

I and all sentient beings have been born in samsara and
    suffered
Numberless times from beginningless rebirths up
    to now.

Our life, this I, these aggregates, our possessions, the people around
us and our family members are all impermanent by nature. They
are impermanent because they are compounded by causes and
conditions and therefore under the control of causes and conditions. That is why everything decays and nothing lasts. Things
change not only day by day, hour by hour, minute by minute and
second by second, but even within each second. Geshe Lamrimpa
from Tibet mentioned that things change even within each second and that this is perhaps the subtlest impermanence.

It is because of not meditating, not being aware and not realizing that phenomena are in the nature of impermanence that
we live our lives with the concept of permanence, believing that
things are going to last for a long time and becoming attached
to them. Then when things do change and death or decay comes
to us or to someone in our family, it is an unbelievable shock.
We have a nervous breakdown or go crazy.

For example, the first time I went to Malaysia I stayed at the
house of a wealthy family because there was no center. Many
lamas had stayed there previously and given the family Buddha statues. I heard that one day the son suddenly died and the
father couldn't stand it. He threw all the statues on the floor
and broke them because he thought that Buddha had not taken
care of his family. That is what happens when you don't think
about impermanence. You think things are permanent and that
you and your family will live for a long time. Then when things
suddenly change, even though that's the nature of life, it is an
unbelievable shock.

LETTING GO OF THE I AND CHERISHING OTHERS

Because of being under the control of these four wrong concepts, we have been suffering since beginningless time and if we continue to follow these wrong concepts, we will experience all these unimaginable sufferings endlessly. Just being free from the ocean of samsaric sufferings and its causes is not enough:

> All sufferings, obstacles, misfortunes and undesirable things come from the self-cherishing thought, from cherishing the I.

It all comes from the self-cherishing thought, from the I.[97] Therefore, the I is something to let go of.

> All happiness—our past happiness from beginningless rebirths, present happiness, future happiness, liberation and enlightenment—comes from the good heart cherishing and wanting to benefit others, bodhicitta.

That means all our past happiness from beginningless rebirths as well as our present and future happiness up to enlightenment comes from others.[98] It comes from numberless hell beings, hungry ghosts, animals, human beings, suras, asuras and intermediate state beings.

Wow! Can you imagine that? All our happiness from beginningless rebirths came from the numberless sentient beings in each realm. Even without thinking of any other happiness, just that much kindness is unimaginable and depthless. There is so much to think about and feel. It is amazing how kind sentient beings are. Each one is unbelievably precious, kind and dear.

97. See note 72 and appendix 6 for the shortcomings of cherishing the self.
98. See note 74 and appendix 6 for the advantages of cherishing others.

On top of that, all our present happiness comes from every hell being, hungry ghost, animal, human being, sura, asura and intermediate state being, therefore they are even more kind, precious and dear.

On top of that, all our future lives' happiness, which is still only temporary happiness, comes from each of the numberless sentient beings in each realm, therefore they are much kinder, much more precious and dear.

On top of that, liberation from samsara comes from each of the numberless hell beings, hungry ghosts, animals, human beings, suras, asuras and intermediate state beings. Wow! Can you imagine? Now this is ultimate happiness, therefore they are unbelievably, unbelievably precious, kind and dear.

On top of that, enlightenment comes from every hell being, hungry ghost, animal, human being, sura, asura and intermediate state being. Wow! Now every sentient being is the dearest, kindest, most precious one in your heart. They are kinder even than Buddha, Dharma and Sangha, because Buddha, Dharma and Sangha came from the kindness of sentient beings. It is like you need food to survive and since the food has to come from a field, that field is very precious.

Therefore, whatever small service and benefit you can offer to anybody, whether it is a person or even an insect that is being eaten or drowning in water, is the happiest, most enjoyable thing in your life. Of course, if you can give great help it is good, but even if you can only offer some small help, still it is the happiest, most meaningful and most joyful thing. By seeing that sentient beings are the most precious, kindest and dearest ones in your life, you are unbelievably happy to do anything you can to help them.

Now think:

I am going to cause sentient beings to have not only the happiness of this life, but more importantly, the happiness of future lives; then even more importantly, ultimate happiness, liberation from samsara; and most importantly, enlightenment. In order to offer that service and benefit to others, I myself must achieve enlightenment. Therefore, I am going to take the eight Mahayana precepts.

Light of the Path

Part 3. The Motivations

When you rise in the morning think deeply from your heart,

"I am going to act in accordance with bodhicitta."

When you go to sleep at night,

Check whether you acted in accordance with or
against bodhicitta.

KHUNU LAMA RINPOCHE[99]

The motivations in this section contain the key points extracted from Rinpoche's teachings. They can be used as a basis to create your own motivations. There is a long version for most of the motivations, followed by a more concise version.

7. Everything Depends on Your Attitude
A Reflection

Think as follows:

MY LIFE HAS BEEN MOST FORTUNATE

My life has been most fortunate. First of all, I have heard the heart of the Buddhadharma, the very essence of the 84,000 teachings of the Buddha, the very precious teaching on the stages of the path to enlightenment many times. I have even heard them from His Holiness the Dalai Lama, who is the real living Chenrezig, the Compassion Buddha manifested in the human form of a monk—the aspect that can most perfectly guide me. Just that alone is most amazing and inexpressible. It is the most unbelievable, rare, fortunate and precious thing that could have happened to me this life.

Then I have met many other great teachers and unbelievably qualified virtuous friends who preserve the whole entire Buddhadharma—the Lesser Vehicle, Mahayana Paramitayana and Mahayana Tantrayana teachings—and who can reveal to me the complete path to enlightenment from their own experience.

So really, if I look at what has happened to me so far this life, it is most amazing.

I CAN'T REALLY TELL WHEN DEATH WILL COME

But of course, this incredible opportunity will not last long. It is just like lightning on a very dark night that for a short time reveals everything clearly and is then gone.

Life is not long and I can't tell when death will come. There are many conditions for death, like the 400 different types of disease, 360 spirit possessions, 1080 interferers and, these days, many new diseases that were never heard of before. Then there is cancer. I hear all the time about this and that friend or family member suddenly getting cancer, but how can I tell that sooner or later other people won't hear my own name with the word "cancer" next to it and a "has" in between? This happens to many people in the world. Already many older students who had been studying Dharma for some time have passed away. I might be next.

I cannot always live my life with the concept of permanence. Life is very short in degenerate times and even things that are supposed to support life can become the condition for death, like medicines having side effects that lead to death or people dying when their house collapses or while eating food.

THE *REAL* MEDITATION IS LAM-RIM

Life is short and there is not much time left, therefore it is extremely important to meditate on the lam-rim. The *real* meditation is lam-rim, the stages of the path to enlightenment.

The great enlightened being Pabongka Dechen Nyingpo mentioned in his teachings that it is more meaningful to spend our lives meditating on lam-rim, the three principal aspects of the path, than to recite many hundreds of millions of OM MANI PADME HUM or other mantras. He also said that it is more meaningful to spend our lives meditating on the lam-rim than even seeing the Buddha. In order to be enlightened I need to achieve all the realizations of the path and that doesn't happen in one second just by seeing Buddha. Of course, by seeing the Buddha I would receive many blessings, but no realizations.

EVERYTHING DEPENDS ON MY ATTITUDE

Lama Tsongkhapa mentioned in his *Mind Training Poem:*

> If you don't purify negative karma and defilements quicker and quicker,
> Being totally under the control of very forceful karma,
> Even though you know this is happiness, that is happiness, you are powerless to choose;
> Even though you know this is suffering, that is suffering, you are powerless to free yourself.
> Therefore, reflect that action and result are non-betraying,
> Look now to choose between white and black karma:
> From this day take care not to create negative karma;
> From this night attend to virtue.
> What better can you do with this life than take care
> Not to create negative karma but instead create virtue all the time?

> White and black actions depend on good and
>   bad thoughts:
> If you have good thoughts, even the paths and
>   grounds are good;
> If you have bad thoughts, even the paths and
>   grounds are bad.
> Everything depends on your attitude.

Because I am under the control of very hard, forceful, powerful karma, if I don't purify all this as quickly as possible, even though I know what is happiness and what is suffering, I am not free to choose. Somehow I just have to go through sicknesses, relationship problems, business problems and so on, powerless to immediately free myself from them.

Once an action is done, karma is created. If the action is non-virtuous, the result will definitely be suffering. If the action is virtuous, the result will definitely be happiness. These results will definitely come. Therefore, I need to reflect on this and then take care not to create negative karma but instead create virtue *all the time.*

Lama Tsongkhapa is saying that everything depends on the mind. Everything depends on my attitude. That is something great to learn—how everything depends on my mind.

For example, if I have a bodhicitta motivation, the good heart benefiting other sentient beings, I can actualize the realizations of the Mahayana path, the five paths and ten grounds.

If I *don't* have a good heart, even if I have renunciation and a realization of emptiness, I can only enter the Lesser Vehicle path and the highest I can achieve is the lower nirvana. I cannot become a bodhisattva and collect skies of merit in every second with every single action of body, speech and mind, as well as purifying all the heavy negative karmas collected in this and past lives. Without bodhicitta, I cannot achieve enlightenment and do perfect work without the slightest mistake for sentient beings, liberating every one of them from the oceans of samsaric suffering and bringing them to enlightenment.

The self-cherishing thought makes my attitude bad. That is why, so far, because of following self-cherishing from beginningless rebirths up to now instead of practicing bodhicitta and benefiting others, I have not been able to achieve the very first realization of impermanence and death, which makes the mind become Dharma, or any other realizations.

My today's self-cherishing thought doesn't allow my actions right now to become a cause of enlightenment, liberation from samsara or the happiness of future lives. It creates so many obstacles even for the happiness of this life and makes things very difficult. Self-cherishing gives rise to attachment to this life, anger and all the other delusions. All obstacles come from the self-cherishing thought.

Since everything comes from your attitude, make the decision to start each day and live your life with bodhicitta.

Light of the Path

8. Cutting the Concept of Permanence

Bodhicitta Motivation for Life 1

The Long Motivation

CUTTING THE CONCEPT OF PERMANENCE

Start by thinking:

Guru Shakyamuni Buddha descended into this world from Tushita Pure Land and showed the twelve deeds of a buddha. He taught the Dharma by expounding the 84,000 teachings and enlightened numberless sentient beings, not only in this world but also in other universes. In this way the benefits to sentient beings were as limitless as the sky.

In the general view, the Buddha turned the Wheel of Dharma three times. He taught the four noble truths in Sarnath, the middle Wheel of Dharma revealing the *Perfection of Wisdom Sutras* at Rajgir and the final Wheel of Dharma teaching the three characteristics at Vaishali. Then the Buddha manifested into Buddha Vajradhara and deities to reveal the tantric teachings. He manifested into Chakrasamvara and revealed the Chakrasamvara teachings on the top of Mt. Meru, into Yamantaka at Orgyen in Pakistan and into Kalachakra at Amaravati in India.

Finally, the Buddha showed impermanence to us sentient beings and passed away into the sorrowless state. All that is left now are scriptures and some ruins at holy places like Rajgir and Sravasti. Therefore, there is no question that I myself can die even today. I *am* going to die today.

Then there were the two close disciples of the Buddha, Shariputra and Maudgalyayana; the Six Ornaments, the pandits Nagarjuna, Asanga, Chandrakirti and so forth; and many other great Indian yogis such as Naropa, Tilopa and Saraha. They wrote many texts, taught and gave unbelievable, incredible benefit to sentient beings and to the teachings of the Buddha in this world. Now I can only hear their names and see the texts they left and some caves and places where they meditated and achieved realizations. Therefore, there is no question that I myself can die even today. I *am* going to die today.

After that, many great lamas appeared in each of the four traditions in Tibet, including Padmasambhava and Longchen Rabjampa; Marpa and Milarepa; the five great Sakya pandits; Lama Tsongkhapa and his disciples, and so forth. They completed the path to enlightenment and gave incredible benefit to sentient beings and to the teachings of the Buddha. Now I cannot see them, just the places where they practiced, like the caves of Lama Tsongkhapa and Milarepa, and their texts, nothing else. They all passed away. Therefore, I myself can die even today. I *am* going to die today.

Even in this life, I have met many virtuous friends who were kinder than all the numberless past, present and future Buddhas and who have passed away. I made a Dharma connection and received teachings from virtuous friends who were great yogis and scholars, but now I cannot see them. Now, those aspects no longer exist. Therefore, I myself can die even today. I *am* going to die today.

Then there were all my family members who passed away, as well as many friends and people I knew who have died. Therefore, I myself can die even today. I *am* going to die today.

So many people who were born on the same day as me in this world and who were the same age have already died. Therefore, I myself can die even today. I *am* going to die today.

Each time you think of death like this, cut your attachment.

So many times I have almost died

Then think:

So many times already in this life, I have almost died. I have almost had a fatal car accident or a fall. Somehow death has not yet come, but if I had died already, by now I would be in the lower realms. By now:

- ▸ I could be a fish caught with a hook in its mouth and sliced alive.
- ▸ I could be a worm pierced by a bird's beak or being eaten by hundreds of ants.
- ▸ I could be in the most terrifying hell realms.

This could happen because I have collected so many causes to be born in the lower realms since beginningless rebirths and they are not yet purified.

Therefore, right now I *must* abandon negative

karma, the cause of suffering, and practice only virtue, the cause of happiness.

Bring it to this conclusion.

Death can come any moment

After that, remember what Nagarjuna explained in the *Precious Garland*:

> Life—*my life*—is like a butter lamp in a strong wind;
> (it can stop any time.)

Therefore, death can come any moment. Meditate on that. Also:

> This life is more impermanent
> Than a water bubble blown by the wind.
> How wonderful it is to be able to wake up from
>   sleep—
> (The fragile state of) simply breathing in and out!

Last night so many people in this world died. They went to bed with many plans for things to do tomorrow, this year, next year and so on. This morning their bodies were corpses.

If I had died last night, by now I would be in the lower realms, because although I did study Dharma and do some practice and retreat, *I didn't engage in continual intensive Dharma practice*. Then anger, ill will and many other things destroyed whatever merits I created.

Therefore, there was no really serious, continual, pure Dharma practice and purification, and if death had come to me last night, by now I would be in those most frightening hell realms.

THE GREAT MEANING OF THIS HUMAN LIFE

Now try to *feel* how incredibly precious this life is:

> How most unbelievably fortunate it is that today I have the freedom to wake up and practice Dharma. In every second there is so much I can do with this human body, not only a precious human body extremely rare to find, but one with eighteen qualities almost impossible to achieve again. Wow!
>
> In each second I have the great freedom and opportunity to create the cause of:
>
> ▸ Happiness in all my future lives—by generating renunciation of this life;
> ▸ Ultimate happiness, liberation from samsara—by generating renunciation of future lives and actualizing the right view;
> ▸ Enlightenment—by generating bodhicitta.
>
> I can create the cause for all of this temporary and ultimate happiness even in one second. Therefore, each second of this perfect human rebirth that I have is much more precious than:
>
> ▸ Mountains of gold and diamonds;
> ▸ Gold and diamonds the size of this earth;
> ▸ The whole sky filled with wish-granting jewels.
>
> Even if I owned skies filled with wish-granting jewels, the value of all that would be nothing compared to one second of this perfect human rebirth, because with all that wealth I still could not achieve the happiness of future lives, liberation from samsara or full enlightenment for sentient beings that I can with this perfect human rebirth.

Therefore, I must not waste even a second of this life! I must make it meaningful by practicing Dharma. Practicing Dharma means:

- Practicing the three principal aspects of the path to enlightenment—renunciation, bodhicitta and right view—as a foundation, and then tantra—abandoning impure appearance and impure thought;
- Living in three levels of vows—pratimoksha, bodhisattva and tantric.

GENERATING BODHICITTA

Now think:

Since I am going to die today, what should I do? I *must* practice bodhicitta.

Begin by reflecting on the shortcomings of cherishing the self, which opens the door to every suffering and obstacle, and on the benefits of cherishing others, which brings all the happiness up to enlightenment to you and to numberless sentient beings, as well as every quality (see appendix 6).

Then do the practice of exchanging self for others, along with the practice of taking and giving. While you are doing taking and giving you can chant the mantra OM MANI PADME HUM.

Taking away the suffering of others

First, do the practice of taking by generating compassion for the numberless sentient beings suffering under the control of delusion and karma. Then take:

- The suffering of the places where they are born;
- All their sufferings;
- The causes of those sufferings, karma and defilements, including the subtle defilements.

Take all of these one by one or all together from each:

- Hell being,
- Hungry ghost,
- Animal,
- Human being,
- Sura,
- Asura,
- Intermediate state being.

Take all of this into your heart and give it to the self-cherishing thought—like putting a bomb on top of your enemy—and completely destroy it. Meditate a little that the truly existent I, the real I that the selfish mind cherishes but which is not actually there, becomes totally non-existent even in name.

You can also take on all the obstacles to:

- Your gurus' holy actions to benefit others according to the view of sentient beings;
- The spreading of the teachings of the Buddha;
- The benefactors who serve the Dharma and the Sangha.

The taking can be done in an elaborate, medium or short way by taking all the sufferings together; it just depends on time.

Giving every happiness to others

For the practice of giving, first generate loving kindness and then give to all the numberless hell beings, hungry ghosts, animals, human beings, suras, asuras and intermediate state beings:

- ▸ All your past, present and future merits;
- ▸ All the resultant happiness of these merits up to enlightenment;
- ▸ All your material possessions and even your family and friends.

Think that by receiving these things, the numberless sentient beings:

- ▸ Receive a perfect human body, meet the Dharma and meet a virtuous friend;
- ▸ Gain perfect enjoyments, perfect companions and are born in a pure land;
- ▸ Actualize the complete path to enlightenment and are liberated from all suffering and its causes;
- ▸ Attain the unimaginable qualities of a Buddha and become the deity you are practicing.

The giving can also be done in an elaborate, medium, short or very short way according to time. Each time you do the practice of taking and giving, you create unimaginable merits and become closer to enlightenment, which means closer to liberating numberless sentient beings.

Concluding prayers

After that, think:

This is just visualization. In reality sentient beings are still suffering. I must liberate them from the oceans of samsaric suffering along with its causes, karma and defilements, and bring them to enlightenment by myself alone. Therefore, I must achieve enlightenment. Therefore, I am going to engage in virtuous activities. May all my activities of body, speech and mind become the cause to achieve enlightenment and enlighten all sentient beings.

Also you can pray:

From now on, may I be like Lama Tsongkhapa, by having the same qualities, and may I be able offer limitless skies of benefit to sentient beings and to the teachings of the Buddha.

Now read and contemplate the *Bodhisattva Attitude*, chapter 10.

The Short Motivation

CUTTING THE CONCEPT OF PERMANENCE

Reflect that death is definite and everyone dies. Even Guru Shakyamuni Buddha and the great pandits and yogis of ancient India and Tibet passed away. Remember your gurus who have passed away, as well as your family members and friends, and think about the many people born on the same day as you who have already died. Make the decision:

> Therefore, I myself can die even today. I *am* going to die today.

Meditate that death can come at any moment. As Nagarjuna said,

> Life is like a butter lamp in a strong wind; (it can stop any time.)

THE GREAT MEANING OF THIS HUMAN LIFE

Now try to *feel* how unbelievably fortunate it is to wake up today with a precious human rebirth that gives every opportunity to practice Dharma. In every second you have the freedom to create the cause of:

- Happiness in all future lives—by generating renunciation of this life.
- Liberation from samsara—by generating renunciation of future lives and actualizing the right view.
- Enlightenment—by generating bodhicitta.

Think:

> Each second of this perfect human rebirth is more precious than even the whole sky filled with wish-granting jewels. Therefore I must not waste even a second, I must make it meaningful by practicing Dharma—living in vows and practicing the three principal aspects of the path along with tantra. Especially, since I am going to die today, I *must* practice bodhicitta.

Generating bodhicitta

Now reflect on the shortcomings of cherishing the self and the benefits of cherishing others (see appendix 6). Then do the practice of exchanging self for others along with giving and taking while chanting OM MANI PADME HUM.

First, generate compassion for the numberless sentient beings in all the six realms suffering under the control of delusion and karma and take into your heart:

- ▸ The suffering of the places where they are born;
- ▸ All their suffering;
- ▸ The causes of that suffering, delusion and karma.

Taking all of this into your heart, destroy your self-cherishing thought completely. Meditate that the truly existent I becomes totally non-existent, even in name. You can also take on obstacles to your gurus' holy actions to benefit others, the spread of the teachings of the Buddha and all the benefactors.

Then generate loving kindness and give to all the numberless beings:

- ▸ All your past, present and future merits;
- ▸ All the resultant happiness of these merits up to enlightenment;

- All your material possessions and even your family members and friends.

Think that by receiving these things they:

- Receive a perfect human rebirth and meet the Dharma and a virtuous friend.
- Gain perfect enjoyments, perfect companions and are born in a pure land.
- Actualize the complete path to enlightenment and are liberated from all suffering.
- Attain the unimaginable qualities of a buddha and become the deity you practice.

After that pray:

> This is just visualization. In reality sentient beings are still suffering. I must liberate them from the oceans of samsaric suffering along with its causes, delusion and karma, and bring them to enlightenment by myself alone. Therefore, I must achieve enlightenment. Therefore, I am going to engage in virtuous activities. May all my activities of body, speech and mind become the cause to achieve enlightenment and enlighten all sentient beings.

You can also pray:

> From now on, may I be like Lama Tsongkhapa by having the same qualities and may I be able offer limitless skies of benefit to sentient beings and to the teachings of the Buddha.

Now read and contemplate the *Bodhisattva Attitude*, chapter 10.

9. Give Up Stretching the Legs

Bodhicitta Motivation for Life 2

The Long Motivation

Go to sleep meditating on the dharmakaya or emptiness. Then, the next morning on waking, rise up from the state of clear light to the sound of the dakas and dakinis playing music and saying,

> Give up stretching the legs.
> Give up entering samsara.
> Generate bodhicitta to achieve Vajrasattva,
>   the Great Victorious One, for all sentient beings.

GIVE UP STRETCHING THE LEGS

Meditate as follows:

> "Give up stretching the legs" means:
>
> > Give up clinging to this life and being too lazy
> > to practice Dharma.
> > Instead, think of impermanence, which is the
> > nature of this life.

Death is definite and can come at any time and any moment, even today. At the time of death nothing can help me except the holy Dharma.

After death, there are only two possible rebirths: a higher rebirth if I have collected virtue or a lower rebirth if I have collected nonvirtue. So far in this life, even though I met the Buddhadharma many years ago, the karma I have collected has been mostly negative. Even in one day I collect mostly negative karma and the negative karmas I create are very powerful because the four parts of the action are more complete. Those actions that become Dharma are extremely rare and they are weaker.

Therefore, if death were to come now, I would definitely be born in the lower realms and I would have to remain there until that karma finishes. Then another karma would ripen bringing another suffering rebirth and it would go on and on like that. It is not sure when I could come back to the human realms.

There is no opportunity to practice Dharma in the lower realms; I would be totally overwhelmed by suffering. I could not benefit myself or others. Therefore, right now while I have this perfect human rebirth qualified with the eight freedoms and ten richnesses, which is so highly meaningful and difficult to find again, I must practice Dharma and I must practice right away.

GIVE UP ENTERING SAMSARA

Now think:

"Give up entering samsara" means:

> Give up thinking that samsara and samsaric
>   pleasures are good and then clinging to them.
> Instead, realize samsara to be suffering as in
>   reality it is only suffering.

Because of always looking at samsara and its pleasures as real, pure happiness, thinking how good they
are and admiring them, attachment arises and then
I enter and engage in samsara. I need to give this up
by looking at samsara as being only in the nature of
suffering.

Samsara is only suffering

Think about the definition of samsara and how this shows samsara is only suffering. Then reflect in more detail on the three
types of suffering:

> The suffering of pain—heat, cold, hunger, thirst and so
> on—is easy to understand. Even animals can recognize
> this as suffering and don't want to experience it.
>
> The suffering of change is far more difficult to realize
> because it includes all samsaric pleasures. I label plea-
> sure on what is really only suffering. I merely impute
> pleasure and then it appears back to my hallucinated
> mind as real pleasure, real pure happiness, but that is
> completely wrong, it is totally non-existent.
>
> Samsaric pleasure is only suffering because it is
> labeled on the feeling when a previous suffering that
> was heavy stopped and a new suffering is beginning
> from small. While that suffering is still small it is unno-
> ticeable and it is labeled "pleasure," but the more sam-
> saric "pleasure" is continued, the more it decreases and
> becomes the suffering of pain again.

All samsaric pleasure is like this, the pleasure decreases as it continues and becomes the suffering of pain. It is because the pleasure is labeled *on* the feeling of suffering that it doesn't last:

- ▸ Samsaric pleasure doesn't increase: as it continues it becomes suffering again.
- ▸ Samsaric pleasure doesn't last: even the pleasure that is generated doesn't last because it is suffering.

Try to get a good understanding of this. Then think:

The *Guru Puja* says,

> Samsara is extremely unbearable like a prison;
> Please bless me to give up looking at it as a very beautiful, happy park.

Because of totally believing that samsara and its pleasures are real happiness, when in reality they are real suffering, I become attached to them and that ties me to samsara with the chain of the twelve dependent related limbs causing me to continuously be reborn in samsara and experience suffering.

It is because of this that I have been suffering from beginningless rebirths up to now, reincarnating again and again and experiencing all the sufferings in each of the six realms as well as the intermediate state. From beginningless rebirths up to now my life has been *totally* under the control of delusion and karma. I have never had a break from the suffering of samsara for even one second.

It is not that I have been constantly experiencing the suffering of pain or the suffering of change, but I have never had a break from pervasive compounding suffering because these aggregates are pervaded by suffering being under the control of delusion and karma. That is why this body and mind are in the nature of suffering all the time.

Also any suffering or happiness that I am experiencing now is nothing new. It may be new for this life, but whatever it is, I have experienced it numberless times in the past. It is just that I can't remember this.

My mind is so blocked, so obscured, that I can't see all the unimaginable sufferings of past lives and I can't see that I will have to go through all the same sufferings in future lives. As my mind is purified, I will gradually be able to remember all the experiences from thousands and billions of past lives. I will also see many hundreds of thousands of lives into the future.

I will see that being in samsara for even a second is like being in the very center of a fire; it is totally scary. I will understand that reincarnating again in samsara is most terrifying. Like a prisoner trapped in his cell, I won't want to be imprisoned even one more minute or one more second. I will only want to be free. To be in samsara is unbelievably, unbelievably sad.

Therefore:

- ‣ Please grant me blessings to give up attachment to the "extremely unbearable prison" of samsara by no longer looking at it as "a very beautiful, happy park."
- ‣ Please grant me blessings to practice the antidote to samsara, the three higher trainings.
- ‣ Please grant me blessings to achieve the result of liberation.

Generate bodhicitta to achieve
Vajrasattva, the Great Victorious One,
for all sentient beings

Now think:

> The reason to "generate bodhicitta to achieve Vajrasattva, the Great Victorious One, for all sentient beings" is as it says in the Kadampa teachings:

>> I is the root of all negative karma; it is to be
>> instantly thrown very far away.
>> Others are the originator of my enlightenment;
>> they are to be immediately cherished.

Think how self-cherishing is the cause of all your problems and the root of all suffering (see appendix 6):

> I is the root of all negative karma; it is instantly to be
> thrown very far away.

Then consider how the I you are cherishing is not actually there because that is the truly existent I that doesn't actually exist. Therefore, it is very foolish and harmful to cherish the I since in reality there is nothing there to cherish. Make the decision that from now on you will cast away self-cherishing as though it were a deadly poison.

Now think how cherishing others brings every happiness:

> Others are the originator of my enlightenment.

> That means not just my friends and those people or
> animals that I like, maybe some cat or dog, but every

single one of the numberless sentient beings in each realm. "Others" are:

- Everybody around me here, right now;
- Every insect, every bird and every worm that I see on the road when I go outside;
- Numberless hell beings and hungry ghosts;
- Numberless animals, big and small, including insects, bugs, mosquitoes, cockroaches, rats, scorpions and all the tiny creatures that live inside the body;
- Numberless human beings—no matter how they look or act;
- Numberless sura, asura and intermediate state beings.

Every single one of these numberless beings is the originator of my enlightenment; therefore, each one is to be immediately cherished, cared for and served with my body speech and mind.

Even if all these sentient beings get angry, criticize or abuse me, don't like me, don't love me, always look down at me and always complain about me, no matter how much I try to help them or how hard I work. Whatever story I may have about them—that their way of thinking is bad or their manner harmful—*still* they are the originator of my enlightenment. No matter what they do, they are the originator of my enlightenment.

And it is not only enlightenment. Every single sentient being is the originator from whom I receive all my numberless past, present and future happinesses:

- Every single temporary pleasure;
- The happiness of all future lives;

▸ Liberation from samsara;
▸ Full enlightenment.

What better gift is there than this?

Then generate bodhicitta by thinking:

> Therefore, in my life there is nothing to do except cherish other sentient beings, work to free them from all the sufferings and their causes and bring them to enlightenment by myself alone. Therefore I must achieve full enlightenment.

Then generate the special tantric motivation to achieve enlightenment, the unified state of Vajradhara, in the quickest way, which is the meaning of Vajrasattva the Great Victorious One:

> From my side, to bring each and every single sentient being to enlightenment, even if I need to be born in the hell realms and suffer for eons equaling the number of drops of the ocean or atoms of this earth, I can do that. But from the side of sentient beings, since they would have to suffer for a most unimaginable amount of time, I need to liberate them from the oceans of samsaric suffering and bring them to enlightenment as quickly as possible. Therefore, I need to achieve enlightenment as quickly as possible. Therefore, from now on I am going to do all the virtuous activities as well as eating, walking, sitting, sleeping, working and so forth, to achieve enlightenment for sentient beings, to liberate them from the oceans of samsaric suffering and bring them to full enlightenment.

And pray to be like Lama Tsongkhapa:

Due to all the past, present and future merits collected by me and by all sentient beings, may I have all the qualities of Lama Tsongkhapa and offer extensive benefit to sentient beings and to the teachings of the Buddha in all my lifetimes.

Now read and contemplate the *Bodhisattva Attitude*, chapter 10.

The Short Motivation

Go to sleep meditating on the dharmakaya or emptiness. Then, the next morning on waking, rise up from the state of clear light to the sound of the dakas and dakinis playing music and saying,

> Give up stretching the legs.
> Give up entering samsara.
> Generate bodhicitta to achieve Vajrasattva,
>   the Great Victorious One, for all sentient beings.

GIVE UP STRETCHING THE LEGS

Think:

> "Give up stretching the legs" means:
>
>> Give up clinging to this life and being too lazy
>>   to practice Dharma.
>> Instead, think of impermanence, which is the
>>   nature of this life.

Remember how precious this human rebirth is and how death can come at any moment. At the time of death a higher rebirth comes only from virtue and a lower rebirth from nonvirtue. Think how often and how easily you create nonvirtue and how powerful those nonvirtues are. Make the decision to give up being lazy and clinging to this life and instead immediately put full effort into practicing Dharma.

GIVE UP ENTERING SAMSARA

Think:

> "Give up entering samsara" means:
>
> > Give up thinking that samsara and samsaric
> > pleasures are good and then clinging to them.
> > Instead, realize samsara to be suffering as in
> > reality it is only suffering.

Now remember the definition of samsara and reflect on how samsara is only suffering. Contemplate the three types of suffering of samsara and particularly the suffering of change. Look at how easily you get attracted and attached to samsaric pleasures which are only in the nature of suffering by wrongly believing they are real happiness. Because of this, you have been reincarnating in samsara continuously up to now, totally under the control of karma and delusion. Your body and mind are in the nature of suffering all the time. Make the determination right now to give up looking at samsara and its pleasures as real happiness and instead work for liberation.

GENERATE BODHICITTA TO ACHIEVE VAJRASATTVA, THE GREAT VICTORIOUS ONE, FOR ALL SENTIENT BEINGS

Think:

> The reason to "generate bodhicitta to achieve Vajrasattva, the Great Victorious One, for all sentient beings" is as it says in the Kadampa teachings:

> I is the root of all negative karma; it is to be
>   instantly thrown very far away.
> Others are the originator of my enlightenment;
>   they are to be immediately cherished.

Think how self-cherishing is the cause of all your problems and the root of all suffering. Then consider how the I you are cherishing is not actually there because that is the truly existent I that doesn't actually exist. Therefore, it is very foolish and harmful to cherish the I since in reality there is nothing there to cherish.

Now think how cherishing others brings every happiness. Every single one of the numberless sentient beings—no matter how they look or what they do—is the originator of all your numberless past, present and future happiness.

Make the decision that from now on you will cast away self-cherishing as though it were a deadly poison and instead only cherish and serve others.

Then generate bodhicitta by thinking,

> In my life there is nothing to do except cherish other sentient beings, work to free them from all the sufferings and their causes and bring them to enlightenment by myself alone. Therefore I must achieve full enlightenment.

And generate the special tantric motivation to achieve enlightenment:

> From my side, to bring each and every single sentient being to enlightenment, even if I need to be born in the hell realms and suffer for eons equaling the number of drops of the ocean or atoms of this earth, I can do that. But from the side of sentient beings, since they

would have to suffer for a most unimaginable amount of time, I need to liberate them from the oceans of samsaric suffering and bring them to enlightenment as quickly as possible. Therefore, I need to achieve enlightenment as quickly as possible. Therefore, from now on I am going to do all the virtuous activities as well as eating, walking, sitting, sleeping, working and so forth, to achieve enlightenment for sentient beings, to liberate them from the oceans of samsaric suffering and bring them to full enlightenment.

Pray to be like Lama Tsongkhapa:

Due to all the past, present and future merits collected by me and by all sentient beings, may I have all the qualities of Lama Tsongkhapa and offer extensive benefit to sentient beings and to the teachings of the Buddha in all my lifetimes.

Now read and contemplate the *Bodhisattva Attitude*, chapter 10.

Light of the Path

10. Bodhisattva Attitude
How to Dedicate Your Life to Others

The Long Motivation

Recite these verses first thing in the morning after generating a bodhicitta motivation for life or at other times. Then contemplate the meaning and keep it in mind throughout the day. (Points for reflection from Rinpoche's commentary are in small type below the relevant verse.)

Giving

I shall give away fully with no sense of loss
My body, enjoyments and all merits of the three times
    (past, present and future)
To accomplish the work for all sentient beings.

As you recite this verse do the meditation on giving. Offer everything from your heart to others with a completely happy mind, just as you would give to the friend closest to your heart or to the person who has been kindest to you in your life. Don't exclude those people you hate even to see or remember; give to "all" sentient beings in order to accomplish the "work" of bringing them the happiness of this life, future lives, liberation from samsara and enlightenment.

If you wish, you can begin the meditation by generating compassion and then taking from the numberless sentient beings:

- All their sufferings.
- All the causes of those sufferings, karma and defilements, including even the subtle defilements.
- The suffering of the places where they live.

Think that all of this absorbs into your ego at your heart and destroys your self-cherishing thought. Also think that having taken this away from sentient beings, they achieve the state of dharmakaya, which is beyond suffering.

Then give:

- All your numberless past, present and future merits and all the resultant happiness that comes from these merits up to enlightenment.
- Your body visualized in the form of numberless wish-granting jewels filling the whole sky.
- All your enjoyments, material possessions and even your family and friends.

Offer all of this to:

- All the numberless hell beings, hungry ghosts, animals, human beings, suras, asuras, intermediate state beings.
- Every arhat and every bodhisattva who is free from samsara.

Think that by receiving all this, they:

- Achieve a pure land where there is no suffering and only beauty. It is filled with wish-granting trees and whatever they wish for happens.
- Receive a perfect human body, meet the Mahayana Dharma and find a perfectly qualified guru who can reveal the path to enlightenment.
- Actualize the complete path to enlightenment in their heart and are liberated from the oceans of samsaric suffering, along with all the causes, delusion and karma, including both the gross and subtle defilements.
- Become enlightened in the form of the deity you are practicing.

Rejoice that you have brought them all to the state of enlightenment.

Death

By giving away all, I will be liberated from the oceans of
samsaric suffering
And my mind will achieve the sorrowless state.
Since I have to leave everything (at death)
It is best to (now) give it away to every single sentient
being.

Sooner or later you will die and at the time of death you will have to leave everything behind. No matter how wealthy or powerful you may be or how many loved
ones surround you, even this body you cherish most will be left behind and only
the bare consciousness will go to the next life. Therefore, it is best to give everything to every single sentient being right now.

Bodhicitta means wanting to be used by others

Having given this body to sentient beings
To use *however* they want that makes them happy,
Whether they always kill me, criticize, beat me or
whatever,
It is totally up to them.

This is very, very important. You must have this thought to actualize or to practice bodhicitta. Bodhisattvas want to be used by sentient beings. The worldly
mind thinks that being used by others is bad, the worst thing, but bodhisattvas
are most happy to accept this. If you want to achieve enlightenment, you have to
practice bodhicitta and this is exactly what the bodhisattvas' attitude is.

The bodhisattvas' attitude is to always totally dedicate their lives day and
night to be used by other sentient beings for their happiness. This is what the
bodhisattva looks for and wishes for all the time. Our motivation should be the
same. If you feel like this, if you are able to change your mind into an attitude
wishing to be used by others for their happiness, there is the opportunity to
gradually become closer and closer to bodhicitta and to have the realization.

It is very important to remember this incredible complete and total change of mind—especially when somebody slaps you! When we do the *Guru Puja* every tsog day there is the practice of taking and giving:

And thus, perfect pure compassionate gurus,
I seek your blessings that all negativities, obscurations and
sufferings of mother migrators
May without exception ripen upon me right now,
And that by giving my happiness and virtue to others
All migrators may experience happiness.

If you do this meditation, you are giving your body, merits and everything to each sentient being. Therefore, how can you get upset when somebody gets angry at you or scolds you? It doesn't make sense! If you remember this taking and giving practice when somebody slaps you, there is no way to get angry back. If you remember all the benefits that you receive from sentient beings—all the numberless past, present and future lives' happiness, liberation and enlightenment—you only want to respect them and give them happiness in return.

This is the reality, but if you listen to the advice of worldly people who don't practice Dharma and if you listen to Western culture, which is based on anger and attachment, then of course it will be different. Worldly people think that if somebody harms you, you should immediately harm them back, even twice as much, or more. Their attitude and behavior is totally opposite to the Dharma and totally opposite to bodhicitta. This point is very important.

Always meaningful for others

Let this body only do actions that cause no harm
    to others,
And whoever looks at or thinks of me,
May it never be meaningless for them.

This prayer is very important. You are praying to be wish-fulfilling for anyone who looks at or thinks of you, not only other people but even animals, insects and spirits. You are praying that just by seeing or remembering you, all their mental and physical sicknesses be healed, that they find faith and devotion in Buddha, Dharma and Sangha, develop compassion, bodhicitta and the good heart, actualize the tantric path and achieve enlightenment.

> Whoever focuses on me—
> Whether with anger or devotion—
> May that always be the cause for them
> To achieve every success.

> May all who say unpleasant things,
> Harm, mock or make fun of me
> Have the fortune to achieve enlightenment.

This is the bodhisattva's attitude. Even if people get angry at you, criticize or beat you, in return pray for that to be the cause for them to achieve whatever happiness and success they seek. This is the best and deepest psychology. No matter how others behave toward you, whether they think badly of you or harm you, in return pray to become wish-fulfilling for them. Pray to become anything that they need.

> May I become a guide for those who are guideless,
> A leader for those who are entering the path,
> A ship, a boat and a bridge
> For all who wish to cross (over water).

> May I become a beautiful garden for those who seek one,
> A light for those who look for light,
> Bedding for those who wish to rest
> And a servant for all who want me as their servant.

Usually our ego wants others to become its servant; here we pray to become a servant for others. This is another total and complete change of our minds into the bodhisattva's attitude.

*The means of living and the cause of happiness for
numberless sentient beings*

Like a wish-granting jewel,
A wish-fulfilling vase, powerful mantra,
Great medicine and a wish-granting tree,
May I fulfill all the wishes of sentient beings.

Just like the sky and the great elements
Earth, (water, fire and wind),
May I always be the means of living and the cause of
    happiness
For sentient beings equaling the limitless sky.

As long as space exists,
As long as sentient beings exist,
May I too abide and eliminate the suffering of sentient
    beings.

Sentient beings use the earth, water, fire, wind and space in so many unimaginable ways for their happiness. Pray to be used by sentient beings exactly like those
great elements in whatever way they want and whatever way is most beneficial
for their happiness. That means not only when your mind is OK and you are in
a good mood, but all the time, even when you are in a bad mood or depressed.
Pray to be used like this always and forever.

The bodhisattva attitude

This bodhisattva attitude makes your life extremely beneficial and meaningful
for sentient beings. It is totally against the ego and totally opposite to the self-
cherishing thought. It diminishes and eliminates the selfish mind that harms you
and harms all sentient beings from life to life.

Generate this motivation in the morning and then remember it throughout the
day. If somebody gets angry, scolds, abuses or says nasty words to you, or if

you ask somebody for help and they refuse, whatever happens, remember this motivation. Then instead of generating anger, delusions and all that junk and garbage, you will have great peace and happiness. You will be free from creating negative karma and in future the result will be enlightenment for you and for all sentient beings.

The Short Motivation

Like a wish-granting jewel,
A wish-fulfilling vase, powerful mantra,
Great medicine and a wish-granting tree,
May I fulfill all the wishes of sentient beings.

Just like the sky and the great elements
Earth, (water, fire and wind)
May I always be the means of living and the cause of
  happiness
For sentient beings equaling the limitless sky.

As long as space exists,
As long as sentient beings exist,
May I too abide and eliminate the suffering of sentient
  beings.

11. Four Wrong Concepts

A Motivation for Taking the Eight Mahayana Precepts

The Long Motivation

Think:

> I and all sentient beings have been suffering in samsara
> from beginningless rebirths up to now because of these
> four wrong concepts.

ONE: LOOKING AT THE AGGREGATES AS BEING THE SELF

> While the aggregates are not I, the self,
> Because of looking at the aggregates as the self
>   and being attached,
> I and all sentient beings have been born and
>   suffered in samsara
> Numberless times from beginningless rebirths
>   up to now.

There is no I, or self, inside this body. (The I or self
are the same thing.) My body is not the self, nor is my
mind. To elaborate:

- Form is not I.
- Feeling is not I.
- Cognition is not I.
- Compounding aggregates are not I.
- Consciousness is not I.

None of these five aggregates is I and even all together they are not the I. The aggregates themselves are not I, nor can I be found *on* the aggregates. Nowhere from the tips of my hair down to my toes can the I or self be found.

There are two things that can't be found:

First, the real I that I believe right now is taking the eight Mahayana precepts: "I am here taking the eight Mahayana precepts." That is the "real" I and it can't be found. "Real" means "*not* merely labeled by the mind" or "existing from its own side" and in reality there is no such thing. Nowhere can that be found.

Second, even the merely imputed I that does exist can't be found. It can be found in this country and right now it can be found here in this place, but it can't be found on these aggregates. If I look for the merely labeled I, I will not find it.

Now focus:

Therefore, this real I that is now taking the eight Mahayana precepts is not there. It can't be found *in* this body or *on* these aggregates. It is totally empty. That I has *total* non-existence from its own side. It is *totally* non-existent right there from where it is appearing to my hallucinated mind.

And:

> This I is *totally* empty not only now, not only from
> last night, not only from birth, but from beginning-
> less time. It has been empty and non-existent from the
> beginning. It never came into existence. But while it
> is like that, I have the hallucination that the I exists
> from its own side.
>
> The I that is just this second merely imputed by
> the mind, the very next second appears back to my
> hallucinated mind as not merely labeled. Then I let
> my mind hold onto that appearance as one hundred
> percent true and in that moment, I create the root of
> samsara, ignorance.

The evolution of samsara and the suffering of the six realms

The reason I hold onto the I as true and create the root
of samsara is because I have been following ignorance
and have been under the control of ignorance from
beginningless rebirths. Ignorance has been my guru
and I have been listening to everything it says with
total trust up to now. Because of that, all the other
negative emotional thoughts and wrong concepts
arise: anger, attachment and ignorance along with all
the many different branches and types of these three
poisonous minds.

Ignorance motivates karma, which plants a karmic
seed on the mere I. From that seed, rebirth is produced.
It is because of this ignorance—the self-grasping of
the person and self-grasping of the aggregates—that
I have been suffering in samsara from beginningless
rebirths up to now:

- Numberless times I have been born in each of the hell realms—the eight major cold hells, the eight major hot hells and the neighboring hells;
- Numberless times I have been born in the hungry ghost realm and experienced the heaviest suffering of hunger and thirst, unable to find a spoonful of food, a drop of water or even dampness on the ground for hundreds, thousands and even tens of thousands of years;
- Numberless times I have been born as an animal and experienced the suffering of being extremely foolish and ignorant, as well as the unbelievably heavy suffering of being eaten alive;
- Numberless times I have been born as a human being and experienced the sufferings of birth, old age, sickness, death, meeting what I don't want, not being able to find what I want, not getting any satisfaction when I do find what I want and the suffering of the aggregates;
- Numberless times I have been born as suras and asuras. The mental suffering I experienced as a sura when nearing death was even heavier than the physical sufferings I experienced as a hell being.

Now think of the three other wrong concepts that come from ignorance:

TWO: LOOKING AT SAMSARIC PLEASURE AS REAL HAPPINESS

While samsaric pleasure is only suffering,
Because of looking at samsaric pleasure as real
    happiness and being attached,

I and all sentient beings have been born and
   suffered in samsara
Numberless times from beginningless rebirths
   up to now.

Samsaric pleasure is only suffering, but because of
labeling it and looking at it as real happiness, and then
being attached, I have been continuously suffering in
samsara from beginningless rebirths up to now.

THREE: LOOKING AT THE BODY AS CLEAN

While this body is dirty,
Because of looking at the body as completely
   clean and being attached,
I and all sentient beings have been born and
   suffered in samsara
Numberless times from beginningless rebirths
   up to now.

My body is like a garbage can or a septic tank that collects all the waste from the toilet. Nagarjuna said the
body is "a container of thirty-six dirty things."

Khunu Lama Rinpoche explained that before food
is eaten, it is clean, but after going inside the body, it
is dirty. Whether it comes out of the mouth, the ears
or the holes in the lower part of the body, it is dirty
because the nature of the body is dirty.

While the nature of my body is dirty, because of
looking at my body as completely clean and being
attached, I have suffered in samsara from beginningless rebirths up to now.

Four: looking at impermanent phenomena as permanent

> While all compounded phenomena are in the
> nature of impermanence,
> Because of looking at compounded phenomena
> as permanent and being attached,
> I and all sentient beings have been born in sam-
> sara and suffered
> Numberless times from beginningless rebirths
> up to now.

My life, this I, these aggregates, my possessions, the people around me and my family members are all impermanent in nature. They are impermanent because they're compounded by causes and conditions and therefore under the control of causes and conditions. That is why everything decays and nothing lasts. Things change not only day by day, hour by hour, minute by minute and second by second, but even within each second. But because of not meditating, not being aware and not realizing that all phenomena are impermanent in nature, I live my life with the concept of permanence and when things change, when death or decay comes to me or someone in my family, it is an unbelievable shock.

Finally, think:

Letting go of the i and cherishing others

Because of being under the control of these four wrong concepts, I and all sentient beings have been suffering since beginningless time. If I continue to follow these wrong concepts, I will have to keep experiencing all these unimaginable sufferings endlessly.

Just myself being free from the ocean of samsaric sufferings and its causes is not enough:

> All sufferings, obstacles, misfortunes and undesirable things come from cherishing the I.

It all comes from the I. Therefore the I is something to let go of.

> All happiness—my past happiness from beginningless rebirths, present happiness, future happiness, liberation and enlightenment—comes from the good heart cherishing and wanting to benefit others, bodhicitta.

That means all my happiness from beginningless rebirths as well as all my present and future happiness up to enlightenment comes from others. It comes from numberless hell beings, hungry ghosts, animals, human beings, suras, asuras and intermediate state beings.

- ► I receive all my past happiness from beginningless rebirths from numberless sentient beings. Therefore, each one is unbelievably precious, kind and dear.
- ► I receive all my present happiness from numberless sentient beings. Therefore, they are even more kind, precious and dear.
- ► I receive all my future lives' happiness from numberless sentient beings. Therefore, they are much kinder, much more precious and dear.
- ► I receive liberation from samsara—which is ultimate happiness—from numberless sentient

beings. Wow! Now, they are unbelievably, unbelievably precious, kind and dear.

‣ I receive enlightenment from numberless sentient beings. Wow! Now every sentient being is the dearest, kindest, most precious one in my heart. They are kinder even than Buddha, Dharma and Sangha, because Buddha, Dharma and Sangha come from the kindness of sentient beings.

Sentient beings are the most precious, kindest and dearest ones in my life. Therefore, anything I can do to help anybody, however great or small the service or benefit, is the happiest, most meaningful, and most joyful thing.

Therefore, in order to cause sentient beings to have the happiness of this life; more importantly, the happiness of future lives; even more importantly, ultimate happiness; and most importantly, enlightenment; I myself must achieve enlightenment. Therefore, I am now going to take the eight Mahayana precepts.

The Short Motivation

Think:

I and all sentient beings have been suffering in samsara
from beginningless rebirths up to now because of these
four wrong concepts:

> While the aggregates are not I, the self,
> Because of looking at the aggregates as the self
>   and being attached,
> I and all sentient beings have been born and
>   suffered in samsara
> Numberless times from beginningless rebirths
>   up to now.

> While samsaric pleasure is only suffering,
> Because of looking at samsaric pleasure as real
>   happiness and being attached,
> I and all sentient beings have been born and
>   suffered in samsara
> Numberless times from beginningless rebirths
>   up to now.

> While this body is dirty,
> Because of looking at the body as completely
>   clean and being attached,
> I and all sentient beings have been born and
>   suffered in samsara
> Numberless times from beginningless rebirths
>   up to now.

> While all compounded phenomena are in the
>   nature of impermanence,
> Because of looking at compounded phenomena
>   as permanent and being attached,

> I and all sentient beings have been born in sam-
> sara and suffered
> Numberless times from beginningless rebirths
> up to now.

If I continue to follow these four wrong concepts, I will experience unimaginable sufferings endlessly. Just myself being free from the ocean of samsaric sufferings and its causes is not enough:

> All sufferings, obstacles, misfortunes and unde-
> sirable things come from cherishing the I.

Therefore the I is something to let go of.

> All happiness—my past happiness from begin-
> ningless rebirths, present happiness, future hap-
> piness, liberation and enlightenment—comes
> from bodhicitta, the good heart cherishing and
> wanting to benefit others.

Therefore other sentient beings are unbelievably precious, kind and dear. To cause the numberless sentient beings to have the happiness of this life, future lives, liberation from samsara and enlightenment, I myself must achieve enlightenment; therefore I am going to take the eight Mahayana precepts.

Part 4. Appendices

If you are going, remember bodhicitta
If you are sitting, remember bodhicitta
If you are lying down, remember bodhicitta
If you are standing, remember bodhicitta.
KHUNU LAMA RINPOCHE[100]

---

100. Op cit., v. 201

Light of the Path

1. How to Start the Day with Bodhicitta

The very first moment when you wake up think, "May all sentient beings achieve full enlightenment." Remember the *Bodhicitta Mindfulness* instructions for waking, rising, dressing, washing, etc. (chapter 4).

Generate bodhicitta by reflecting on one of the motivations for life, either the longer *Cutting the Concept of Permanence* (chapter 8) or the more concise *Give Up Stretching the Legs* (chapter 9). Then recite and contemplate the *Bodhisattva Attitude* (chapter 10).

You can also contemplate *A Direct Meditation on the Stages of the Path to Enlightenment* (appendix 2) or, when taking the eight Mahayana precepts, *Four Wrong Concepts* (chapter 11).

Either before or after the motivations, recite the *Morning Mantras* (appendix 3). Then continue with Thirty-five Buddhas, guru yoga and your own practices.

Try to maintain the bodhicitta motivation, bodhisattva attitude and bodhicitta mindfulness practices throughout the day.

Light of the Path

2. A Direct Meditation on the Stages of the Path to Enlightenment[101]

Perfected with All the Important Points of the Path to Enlightenment

---

This short lam-rim prayer can be used as an alternative morning motivation before reciting the *Bodhisattva Attitude*. It contains the essence of the whole path to enlightenment and reciting it mindfully leaves a positive imprint in the mind to actualize all the realizations. It also directs your life to achieve enlightenment for sentient beings as quickly as possible by practicing the path of the three capable beings and especially Highest Yoga Tantra.

A DIRECT MEDITATION ON THE STAGES OF THE PATH TO ENLIGHTENMENT

Correctly devoting to the spiritual friend

Nature that embodies all the buddhas,
Source of all the pure transmission and realization Dharma,
Principal amongst all the arya sangha:
I take refuge in all magnificent pure gurus.

101. This prayer was composed by Vajradhara Losang Jinpa, translated by Ven. Thubten Dekyong and edited by Maureen O'Malley, Ven. Ailsa Cameron, Ven. Connie Miller and Nick Ribush. The present version has been reformatted by the editor on the basis of a commentary given by Rinpoche on 7 October 2010, Shedrup Ling. The short introduction to the prayer is also summarized from the same commentary.

Please bless my mind to become Dharma,
That Dharma to become the path,
And that path to be free of all hindrances.
Until I achieve enlightenment, may I,
Just like the bodhisattvas, Sudhana and Sadaprarudita,
Practice pure devotion to my guru in thought and action,
See all the actions of my guru as excellent,
And fulfill whatever he advises.
Please bless me with the potential to accomplish this.

The path of the lower capable being

Knowing that this highly meaningful perfect human rebirth
Is difficult to obtain and easily lost,
Realizing the profundity of cause and effect
And the unbearable sufferings of the lower realms,
From my heart I take refuge in the three precious sublime ones,
Abandon negativity, and practice virtue in accordance with the
    Dharma.
Please bless me with the potential to accomplish this.

The path of the middle capable being

In dependence on this, I am able to attain
Only the higher rebirths of humans and gods.
Not having abandoned afflictions,
I have to experience uninterrupted, limitless cyclic existence.
By contemplating well how cyclic existence works,
May I train day and night in the principal path
Of the three precious higher trainings—
The means of attaining liberation.
Please bless me with the potential to always train like this.

The path of the higher capable being

In dependence on this, I am able to attain only self-liberation.
As there is not one sentient being in all the six realms
Who has not been my mother or father,
I will turn away from this lower happiness
And generate the wish to fulfill their ultimate purposes.
By contemplating the path of equalizing and exchanging self
     for others,
I will generate the precious bodhicitta
And engage in the bodhisattvas' actions of the six perfections.
Please bless me with the potential to train in this way.

The path of the Secret Mantra Vajrayana of the higher capable being

Having trained like this in the common path,
I myself will not have aversion to experiencing
The sufferings of cyclic existence for a long time,
But by the force of extraordinary unbearable compassion for
     sentient beings,
May I enter the quick path of the Vajrayana.
By observing purely my vows and pledges even at the cost of
     my life,
May I quickly attain the unified state of Vajradhara
In one brief lifetime of this degenerate age.
Please bless me with the potential to attain this.

Now read and contemplate the *Bodhisattva Attitude*, chapter 10.

Light of the Path

3. Morning Mantras (Concise)[102]

Taking the Essence at the Start of Each Day

Recite the following mantras at the start of each day on waking, either before or after contemplating one of the bodhicitta motivations for life. Buddha taught these mantras out of compassion to increase our virtue and help make our lives as meaningful as possible each day by directing it to enlightenment.

Increasing effect mantra

OM SAMBHARA SAMBHARA BIMANA SARA MAHA JAVA HUM / OM SMARA SMARA BIMANA SKARA MAHA JAVA HUM (7X)

Reciting this mantra seven times increases any virtue created during the day 100,000 times. This mantra comes from the *Sutra of the Complete Dedicated Chakra*.

Mala blessing mantra

OM RUCHIRA MANI PRAVARTAYA HUM (7X)

Recite this mantra seven times and then blow over the mala. By doing this, whatever mantra you recite that was taught by the Buddha, the Tathagata, will

---

102. These mantras can be found in the *FPMT Retreat Prayer Book*, pp. 7–11. The version found here is based on Rinpoche's commentary at *Light of the Path*, 11 and 12 September 2009.

increase more than one hundred billion times. This is taught in the *Sutra of the Unfathomable Celestial Mansion Developing the Jewel.*

Mantra for blessing the feet

OM KHRECHA RAGHANA HUM HRI SVAHA (7x)

Recite this mantra three or seven times and spit on the soles of your feet or shoes. Then any insect that dies under your feet during the day will be born in the Thirty-three deva realm. This is from the *Manjugosha Root Tantra.* You can also spit on the tires of your car and so forth.

Mantra to increase the power of recitations

TADYATHA OM DHARE DHARE BENDHARE SVAHA (7x)

Reciting this mantra seven times before reciting Dharma texts or *sadhanas* increases the power of your recitation ten million times. Reciting it in the morning will increase the merit of whatever recitations you do during the day.

Blessing the speech[103]

I go for refuge to the three precious sublime ones
   (Buddha, Dharma, Sangha).
May I achieve enlightenment to benefit transmigrating
   beings. (3x)

Purify in emptiness. Out of emptiness, your wisdom understanding emptiness manifests as the deity with whom you have a kar-

---

103. This practice for *Blessing the Speech* comes from the great yogi Khyungpo. A direct translation of this with notes can be found in *FPMT Retreat Prayer Book*, p. 8. The version printed here is adapted from Rinpoche's commentary, which elaborates on the meditation.

mic connection.[104] Above your tongue is the syllable AH, which transforms into a moon disc. At its center stands a white OM. Starting from the front of the OM and circling clockwise is ALI, the white vowels:

OM A AA I II U UU RI RII LI LII E AI O AU AM AH SVAHA

Outside of and around that, starting from the front of the OM and circling counterclockwise is KALI, the red consonants:

OM KA KHA GA GHA NGA / CHA CHHA JA JHA NYA / TA THA DA DHA NA / TA THA DA DHA NA / PA PHA BA BHA MA / YA RA LA VA / SHA SHA SA HA KSHA SVAHA

Starting from the front of the OM and circling clockwise around that is the blue heart of dependent arising mantra:

OM YE DHARMA HETU PRABHAVA HETUN TESHAN TATHAGATO HYAVADAT TESHAN CHAYO[105] // NIRODHA EVAM VADI MAHA SHRAMANA YE SVAHA

Beams emitted from the mantra garlands hook back the blessing power of the holy speech of all the buddhas and bodhisattvas in the form of many vowels, consonants and heart of dependent arising mantras and the eight auspicious signs, seven perfect royal objects and eight substances. These absorb to the mantras on your tongue.

Then the beams hook back the blessing power of all the yogis and accomplished ones on the various grounds of the path both beyond and within samsara and all the sages who have achieved

104. Generating as the deity is for those who have received an initiation.
105. Rinpoche emphasizes the need to stop between the YO and NI; otherwise the mantra has a totally different and unintended meaning.

the words of truth[106] in the form of the vowels, consonants and heart of dependent arising mantras and the eight auspicious signs, seven perfect royal objects and eight substances, which absorb to the mantras on your tongue.

Now recite the vowels, consonants and mantra of the heart of dependent arising mantra three times each, pronouncing the syllables very clearly and visualizing as follows:

As you recite the vowels three times, white nectar beams are emitted from each of the white syllables, completely filling your whole body, purifying all the negative karmas of your body and defilements collected from beginningless rebirth up to now:

OM A AA I II U UU RI RII LI LII E AI O AU AM AH SVAHA

As you recite the consonants three times, red nectar beams are emitted, completely filling your whole body, purifying all the negative karmas of your speech and defilements collected from beginningless rebirth up to now:

OM KA KHA GA GHA NGA / CHA CHHA JA JHA NYA / TA THA DA DHA NA / TA THA DA DHA NA / PA PHA BA BHA MA / YA RA LA VA / SHA SHA SA HA KSHA SVAHA

As you recite the mantra of the heart of dependent arising three times, blue nectar beams are emitted, completely purifying all the negative karmas of your mind and defilements collected from beginningless rebirth up to now:

106. Tib: *Drang-song den-tshig drub-pa*, "sages who accomplished the words of the truth." These can be worldly beings but because they live their life in silence, abstaining from gossip and telling lies and so forth, their words have great power and their prayers are more quickly actualized.

OM YE DHARMA HETU PRABHAVA HETUN TESHAN
TATHAGATO HYAVADAT TESHAN CHAYO // NIRODHA
EVAM VADI MAHA SHRAMANA YE SVAHA

This visualization can be done one by one or all together.

When you finish reciting the mantra:

- The heart of dependent arising mantra absorbs into the consonants, KALI.
- The consonants absorb into the vowels, ALI.
- The vowels absorb into the OM.
- OM absorbs into the moon disc.
- The moon disc absorbs back into the syllable AH.
- The syllable AH melts into white-red nectar and absorbs into your tongue.
- Then your tongue becomes the nature of the vajra, indestructible. No matter what food you eat, it is impossible for you to lose the power of your speech.

Then think, "My speech has become perfect. All the blessing power of the buddhas and bodhisattvas speech has now entered my speech." Then recite this dedication prayer:

> May my tongue achieve the power[107] of the Ones Gone to Bliss (the buddhas).
> By the power of the magnificence of my words,
> May all sentient beings be subdued.[108]
> Whatever words I say, may their meaning be accomplished immediately.[109]

107. "Power" could also be "courage."
108. You are praying here that whenever you teach or talk to others your speech can help them and bring them inner peace by pacifying their delusions, selfish mind, negative thoughts and so forth.
109. This means not just when you are teaching Dharma but also at other times

Reciting the prayer for blessing the speech (1) makes your speech perfect, (2) increases the power of your mantra recitation ten million times, (3) stops the power of your speech being taken away by eating black foods, and (4) transforms whatever you say—even gossiping—into virtue, like reciting a mantra.

It is said that Nagarjuna's heart practice was to recite these vowels, consonants and the heart of dependent arising mantra after engaging in any virtuous activities of body, speech and mind. Chanting these three after any mantra recitation makes that recitation more powerful and accomplishes the purpose for which you are reciting the mantra.

Arya Totally Pure Stainless Beam mantra

NAMA NAWA NAWA TEENEN TATHAAGATA GANGA NAM DIVA LOKAA NEN / KOTINI YUTA SHATA SAHA SRAA NEN / OM VOVORI / TSARI NI TSARI / MORI GOLI TSALA WAARI SVAHA (a few times)

This mantra has many benefits.[110] For example, if you recite this mantra in the morning, any person or animal who hears your voice, touches you or is touched by your shadow will have their very heavy negative karma of having committed the five negative karmas without break in this or past lives purified.

Mantra taught by Buddha Droden Gyälwa Chhö

OM HRI YA DHE SARVA TATHAAGATA HRIDAYA GARBE / ZOLA DHARMA DHATU GARBE / SANGHA HARANA AYU SANGSHODHAYA / PAPAM SARVA TATHAAGATA SAMEN-DRA AUSHNI KHA VIMALE BISHUDHE SVAHA (a few times)

---

when you are talking to others or asking them to do something, may whatever you say be accomplished.

110. For a full list of the benefits of this and the following mantra translated and compiled by Rinpoche, see *Taking the Essence All Day and Night*, pp. 57–9.

Again, there are many benefits to this mantra.[111] For example, by reciting this, any of the four elements you touch—earth, water, air, fire—become blessed and able to purify the very heavy negative karma of any sentient being who touches them.

111. ibid. pp. 61–63.

Light of the Path

4. Bodhicitta Mindfulness (Concise)[112]

How to Live Your Life for Numberless Sentient Beings

This is a concise version of the bodhicitta mindfulness practices compiled by Lama Zopa Rinpoche. Rinpoche strongly encourages us to use them in both retreat and daily life.

Mindfulness practice can be related to all the different parts of the lam-rim—renunciation, bodhicitta and right view—as well as tantric practice. These bodhicitta mindfulness practices make our lives highly meaningful because they keep our minds in bodhicitta. Many of them relate to the daily activities we engage in all the time. By doing these everyday actions with the motivation of bodhicitta—dedicating them for the happiness of all sentient beings—they all become the purest Dharma and the cause of enlightenment. This brings the greatest benefit to us, those around us, the world and all sentient beings.

These mindfulness practices come from the *Sutra of the Clouds of the Sublime Rare Ones* (*mdo-sde dkon-mchog-sprin*), Rinpoche, his gurus and other sources; here they are presented together. Also included are concise instructions for the yogas of

112. This collection of bodhicitta mindfulness practices is based on teachings given at the 100 Million Mani Retreat, May 2009, *Light of the Path*, September 2009, and Most Secret Hayagriva Retreat, March 2010. Revisions have been made on the basis of subsequent teachings at *Light of the Path*, 22 September 2010, 7 October 2010, Shedrup Ling, and Lama Zopa Rinpoche Australia Retreat, 8 April 2011.

sleeping, cleaning, eating, bathing and walking, as well as offering incense and going to the toilet.

BODHICITTA MINDFULNESS

Whoever seeks liberation, the state of omniscience, for the sake of each and every one of the numberless sentient beings needs to purify defilements and collect merits in many different ways. Therefore, the Omniscient One, who is extremely skilful and has great compassion for us sentient beings, has shown methods to collect inconceivable virtue even by way of doing our normal daily activities. The Buddha has revealed these methods to benefit those of us whose level of mind is lower[113] so that everything we do is dedicated to be the cause of happiness for all sentient beings.[114]

In the morning, the very first moment when you wake up, think:

May all sentient beings achieve the holy body of the Buddha.[115]

---

113. Those who have not yet generated the actual realization of bodhicitta and whose level of mind is therefore "lower" than the bodhisattvas who have generated bodhicitta.

114. This passage is always translated by Rinpoche as an introduction to the bodhicitta mindfulness teachings but I am not clear as to its source.

115. The Buddha has two holy bodies—dharmakaya and rupakaya. Thinking this way when you wake up and wishing all sentient beings to achieve enlightenment is the shortest way to set a motivation.

Every time you rise—getting up from bed, standing up after sitting and so forth—think:

> May all sentient beings rise up from the great oceans
> of samsaric suffering.

When you get dressed:

> May all sentient beings clothe themselves with shyness
> and shame.[116]

If you are practicing tantra, offer all the clothing as divine dress to yourself as the guru-deity. In tantric practice, as mentioned in the commentaries, all activities—washing, dressing, eating and so forth—become guru yoga because everything is done as an offering to yourself as the guru visualized in the aspect of the deity. By thinking you are offering to the guru, you collect the highest, most extensive merit.

When you tie your belt:

> May all sentient beings' minds be bound by the three
> higher trainings (moral conduct, concentration and
> wisdom).

---

116. Rinpoche uses "shyness" to refer to oneself and with the meaning of being concerned to protect one's vows because of not wanting to create negative karma and suffer but wanting to achieve realizations, and "shame" to refer to others with the meaning that there is a concern to protect the vows one has promised to keep in the presence of holy beings and out of consideration for others. However, other translators commonly use "shame" in reference to oneself and "embarrassment" or "consideration" in reference to others.

When you release your belt:

> May all sentient beings be freed from the bondage of delusion and karma.

Every time you sit down:

> I will lead all sentient beings to the heart of enlightenment. May this happen.

Think this, take on the responsibility and also pray for it to happen.

When you lie down in bed:

> I will bring all sentient beings to the sorrowless state (great liberation or enlightenment).

As you go to sleep:

> May all sentient beings achieve the dharmakaya.

When you offer incense:

> May the bad smell of all sentient beings' stains of wicked nature be eliminated and may they have the scented smell of morality.[117] May they live in pure morality.

> (Or:) May all sentient beings have pure morality.

---

117. Rinpoche explains that some holy beings have this special natural scented smell as a sign of their pure moral conduct or bodhicitta.

In general, when making any offering, you can, of course, generate the motivation, "I am going to free all sentient beings from the oceans of samsaric suffering and bring them to enlightenment, therefore I am going to make this offering," but the specific dedication for incense is to purify and eliminate the impure moral conduct of all sentient beings. Offering incense is a special cause to be able to live in pure morality in future lives, which is the basis of achieving realizations. Therefore it is good to offer a lot of incense and as you light it, dedicate in this way.

When you clean:

> May all sentient beings not have bad conduct. May
> they have perfect, beautiful conduct.

Clean the place where you have holy objects regularly, whether it is dirty or not, thinking that you are cleaning away all sentient beings' disturbing thought obscurations and subtle defilements. The brush, vacuum, broom and so forth are the antidote to those obscurations—the complete path of method and wisdom, from guru devotion up to enlightenment.

In the lam-rim, when cleaning we recite "Abandon dust and abandon stains." Here, "dust" refers to the disturbing thought obscurations that mainly interfere with achieving liberation and "stains" refers to the subtle obscurations that interfere with achieving enlightenment. This is mainly related to oneself, but in the bodhicitta mindfulness practices everything is related to other sentient beings.

Every time when you wash anything—your face, clothing, pots, laundry and so forth—or even brush your teeth:

> I am washing away all the stains of the delusions of
> all sentient beings.

Think that the toothbrush, toothpaste, water, soap and so forth are the complete graduated path to enlightenment and that you are cleaning away every obscuration from all sentient beings' minds. This way, because you are dedicating for all sentient beings, you create limitless skies of merit with each stroke of the brush as you clean your teeth.

There is always so much washing up to be done in the kitchen after eating. By habituating yourself to this way of thinking, all your activities of washing become the cause of enlightenment. Remember to dedicate for all sentient beings—not just those you love but everybody, including your enemy. Then the action becomes Dharma and you can really enjoy it. By dedicating to wash away all the delusions of others, naturally your own delusions are purified.

Whenever you wash or bathe yourself there are *outer, inner* and *secret washing*:

- ▸ For *outer washing*, first bless the water in a bucket or tub by chanting a few of the five powerful mantras that purify negative karma[118]—Namgyalma, Mitukpa, Kunrig, Stainless Lotus Pinnacle and the Wish-Granting Wheel mantra—as well as OM MANI PADME HUM and then blowing on the water. This makes the water very powerful and as you wash your negative karma is purified. It also good for healing.

- ▸ For *inner washing*, if you have received a great initiation from the lower tantra, such as the Great Chenrezig, or an initiation of highest tantra, generate yourself as the deity and think that empowering deities are pouring vase water over your head purifying all your delusions and granting initiation.

---

118. See *Taking the Essence All Day and Night*, pp. 65–67.

▸ *Secret washing* is done in Highest Yoga Tantra according to the instructions of the deity you are practicing.

In all these cases, dedicate your washing for the obscurations of all sentient beings to be cleared away.

You can also visualize making a bath offering to your guru as you wash. If you have received an initiation, generate yourself as the guru-deity, and if not, visualize your root guru at your heart. Then, while bathing, recite the long, medium or short verses of the *Jor-chö* bath offering practice.[119]

To do the bath offering in a short way, as you wash, keep on reciting this offering verse to the guru:[120]

Guru Vajradhara, encompassing all the three objects of
refuge,
Manifesting in the form of a virtuous friend for
whomever it subdues,
Granting the common and sublime realizations,
To the kind guru, I offer this bath.

When you blow your nose, think:

I am clearing away all sentient beings' negative karma
and delusion.

When you enter a temple or even your own house or meditation room:

May all sentient beings be led into the city of the sorrowless state (great liberation or enlightenment). May they enter the city of liberation.

119. *FPMT Retreat Prayer Book*, pp. 65–70. The verses include not just washing but also drying and dressing and for lay people (pp. 71–72) wearing perfume and ornaments.
120. ibid. p. 67.

Pray like this. Think that you are actually doing it and dedicate for it to happen.

When you go out:

> I am liberating all sentient beings from the prison of samsara bound by delusion and karma. May this happen.

When you open any door:

> I am opening the door of the transcendental wisdom gone beyond samsara for all sentient beings. May this happen.

When you close the door:

> I am closing the door of samsara for all sentient beings. May this happen.

Each time you meet your guru:

> May every sentient being meet a perfectly qualified guru who reveals the complete path to enlightenment.

When you see a stupa:

> May all sentient beings achieve the dharmakaya.

The minute you see any holy object or buddha statue:

> May all sentient beings achieve enlightenment quickly.

(Or:) May all sentient beings see the pure land of Buddha.

(Or:) May all sentient beings achieve the three kayas[121] *or* the three vajras.[122]

When you make a fire:

I am burning all sentient beings' delusions in the fire of transcendental wisdom.

While you are cooking food in a pot, if you have received a Highest Yoga Tantra initiation you can use the same meditation that is used for blessing the inner offering. Then when the food is ready, it is already blessed and you can just eat it.

When you eat food:

May all sentient beings be free of the six root delusions and twenty secondary delusions.

When you eat, transform your eating into eating yoga,[123] otherwise the eating becomes ordinary and, if done with attachment, the cause of samsara and the lower realms.

There are three things to be done when eating:

1. Make offering to Buddha, Dharma, Sangha by blessing the food and using the food offering meditation and prayers.
2. Make charity to all sentient beings. Make charity to the 21,000 beings living in your body in order to make a

---

121. The three holy bodies of a buddha—dharmakaya, sambhogakaya, rupakaya.
122. The vajra holy body, speech and mind of a buddha.
123. See "The Yoga of Offering Food" in *Taking the Essence*, pp. 40–54.

connection with them, so that in the future when they become human you can reveal Dharma to them and bring them to enlightenment.

Also, after you finish blessing and offering the food to Buddha, Dharma and Sangha, make charity of the food to numberless hell beings, hungry ghosts, animals, humans, suras and asuras. Think that they are fully satisfied and generate the complete path to enlightenment and that every one of them becomes the deity.

3. Practice eating yoga. In Hinayana, food is eaten without attachment to sustain the body in order to practice Dharma. In Mahayana Paramitayana, food is eaten seeing oneself as a servant and other sentient beings as the master. One then eats in order to be able to serve them. In Mahayana Tantrayana practice, food is offered to oneself generated as the guru-deity.

In Highest Yoga Tantra, the food is blessed into nectar and then taken in either of two ways:

- As a tsog offering to yourself as the guru in the aspect of the deity by offering the nectar to the seed syllable at your heart or to the deity's body mandala (if there is one).
- In the manner of doing "burning offering" practice.

With either of these meditations, each bite of food creates the highest most extensive merit and eating becomes the quickest path to enlightenment. If, after taking a Highest Yoga Tantra initiation, you do not bless your food and take it in one of these two ways, it becomes pollution, like poison.

If you have not received any initiations you can still visualize offering your food as nectar to your root guru at your heart and generating great bliss.

When you are cutting anything, for example, slicing vegetables, chopping wood and so forth:

> May all sentient beings' root of samsara—the ignorance holding on to the I as truly existent—be cut by the sword of the wisdom realizing emptiness.

> (Or:) I am cutting all sentient beings' self-cherishing thought with the knife of bodhicitta.

When you are walking, follow Milarepa's advice that, "When I walk, I have an instruction that makes walking circumambulation." Think that all holy objects in all ten directions are on your right side and that as you walk you are circumambulating them. This purifies past negative karma and creates the cause for enlightenment.

Do the same when you are driving a car, riding a bicycle, traveling on a bus, train and so forth.

You can also remember the pure land where you wish to be reborn and think:

> I am bringing all sentient beings to Buddha's pure land.

This makes it easy to be born in a pure land when you die. Or you can think:

> I am bringing all sentient beings to enlightenment.

When you are descending, like walking downhill, think:

> I am going down to liberate the sentient beings in the lower realms.

When you go to the toilet:

- Visualize Vajrasattva on your crown.
- Recite the long or short Vajrasattva mantra twenty-one times or as many as you can and imagine nectar beams descending and purifying all sentient beings on a moon disc at your heart.
- Think that all the defilements and negative karmas, spirit harms, obscurations and sicknesses—such as cancer—of yourself and all sentient beings collected since beginningless rebirths come out from below and are transformed into nectar that enters into the mouth of the Lord of Death nine storeys down below the earth.

Think that the Lord of Death is fully satisfied. As you flush and close the lid of the toilet, imagine his mouth closes and is sealed with a very heavy, golden double vajra.

5. Prayer of St Francis[124]

The prayer commonly attributed to St. Francis is included here in a version adapted by Rinpoche because of its similarity with the *Bodhisattva Attitude*.

PRAYER OF ST. FRANCIS

Lord (Buddha), make me an instrument of your peace.
Where there is hatred, let me sow love.
Where there is injury, pardon.
Where there is discord, unity.
Where there is doubt, faith.
Where there is error, truth.
Where there is despair, hope.
Where there is sadness, joy.
Where there is darkness, light.

O divine master,
Grant that I may not so much seek to be consoled (happiness
    for the ego) as to console;
To be understood as to understand;
To be loved as to love.

124. Rinpoche adapted this prayer for inclusion in a special booklet to be given to students newly receiving the refuge vows. This version is taken from *Essential Buddhist Prayers, Volume 1*.

For it is in giving that we receive;
It is in pardoning that we are pardoned;
It is in dying (having practiced) that we are born to eternal life
  (from happiness to happiness up to full enlightenment).

6. The Shortcomings of Cherishing the Self and the Advantages of Cherishing Others[125]

Points for Reflection

THE SHORTCOMINGS OF CHERISHING THE SELF[126]

First consider how all your present problems are directly related to the self-cherishing thought. Think, for example, that it is because of self-cherishing that:

- I come into conflict, quarrel and argue with others and get upset when criticized or shown disrespect.
- I suffer from stress, loneliness and depression.
- I experience the pain of anger when others don't do what I want or go against my wishes.
- I experience the pain of attachment and rejection over and over again.
- I suffer from jealousy toward those who have what I want or more than I do; competitiveness toward those I regard as equals; and arrogance toward those I regard as inferior.
- I see others as enemies, break up with friends, and go against my teachers, parents, relatives and even my

---

125. From *Compassion Training*.
126. See also "The Third Power: Blaming the Ego," *Practicing the Five Powers near the Time of Death*.

spiritual friends, who only ever do what is best for me.

- I find it so hard to find time to meditate, to follow the guru's advice, to train my mind in the path, to generate loving-kindness and compassion for others and help them, and to create the causes for future happiness up to enlightenment.

- I constantly follow my old habitual bad habits seeing them as my friends and blaming others for my problems.

- Even when I do generate good qualities, they become corrupted by pride.

Then consider how all your problems come from negative karma motivated by self-cherishing in the past. (This includes all sicknesses, harms and mental and physical suffering, which are the result of negative thoughts and actions created in the past due to the self-cherishing attitude.) Think how in the past self-cherishing has:

- Kept me locked in the prison of samsara for numberless lives since beginningless time, compelling me to bear the sufferings of the six realms as much as possible.

- Kept me in ignorance, continuously obsessed by countless problems.

- Prevented every opportunity to achieve enlightenment.

- Stopped me from receiving any realizations.

- Prevented me from understanding and practicing the Dharma.

- Not even allowed the enjoyment of temporal happiness.

Finally, recognize how self-cherishing is the source of all problems and will only continue to cause harm in the future:

- Self-cherishing has harmed me in the past, is harming me now and, unless I put an end to it, will constantly harm me again in the future. It is my worst enemy and prevents all my happiness.
- In fact, all the problems and suffering in this world, from the smallest conflict to the largest war, come from the self-cherishing thought.

By analyzing in this way, it becomes clear that self-cherishing is something to be immediately abandoned.

THE ADVANTAGES OF CHERISHING OTHERS

Start by considering how cherishing others prevents all the previous sufferings that arise from self-cherishing and motivates you to abandon nonvirtue and practice virtue, which brings happiness as a result. Think, for example, that by cherishing others:

- I abandon killing and harming and practice protecting life and caring for others, which is the cause for a long life, perfect health and great happiness.
- I abandon stealing and miserliness and practice generosity, which is the cause of wealth and enjoyments.
- I abandon anger and intolerance and become patient, loving and kind, which is a cause for great beauty of body and mind.

Then consider the difference between yourself and the Buddha:

In the past we were the same, both just ordinary sentient beings. Then, because the Buddha renounced the self-cherishing thought and generated the mind cherishing others he achieved supreme enlightenment, free of all suffering and able to help all beings.

I, on the other hand, clung on to my self-cherishing

attitude and remain stuck in samsara not even capable of helping myself.

The reason I am unable to do any of the activities of the great bodhisattvas is because I haven't given up self-cherishing and learned how to cherish others. Every good thing comes from cherishing others more than myself.

Now consider how everything you have and enjoy this life comes through the kindness of others because:

- My body comes from the kindness of my parents who bore so many hardships for me.
- My education comes from the kindness of those who taught me.
- My money comes from the kindness of those who employ and pay me.
- My clothes come from the kindness of those who make them as well as from those sentient beings whose wool, fur and skin are used as fabric.
- My food comes from the kindness of those who grow it and those creatures who lose their lives when it is being produced.
- My home, office and so forth come from the kindness of those who built them.
- All the material things I have and enjoy and even non-material things, like being praised, having a good reputation, receiving affection and so forth, come from others.

Thinking more deeply about the kindness of others:

- This precious human life with many qualities comes from the kindness of others because I depend on them to create the causes to receive it—ethics, generosity and patience.

- ▸ The happiness of future rebirths comes from the kindness of others because I need others in order to create the causes for this, such as abandoning the ten nonvirtues and practicing the ten virtuous actions.
- ▸ The everlasting happiness of liberation depends on the kindness of others because the basis for achieving this is ethics, which means living in precepts and avoiding harming others.
- ▸ The peerless, ultimate happiness of enlightenment comes from the kindness of others because it comes from bodhicitta, which comes from great compassion, which is generated by cherishing every single being. Also I need others to practice the six perfections and four ways of gathering disciples. For example, it is through the kindness of those who criticize and harm me that I develop patience and so forth.
- ▸ The Buddha, Dharma and Sangha in whom I take refuge come from sentient beings because without sentient beings there would be no Buddha. Buddha achieved enlightenment because of cherishing sentient beings and then appeared on this earth and taught the Dharma for sentient beings.

Also remember that all this kindness has been shown to you not just this life but over countless past lifetimes. Sentient beings have also been your mother countless times in the past and kind to you in numberless ways[127] and the kindness will continue endlessly in the future.

By thinking over all these reasons, it becomes clear that sentient beings are the source of all your happiness and are like an inexhaustible field for accumulating endless virtue or a jewel that fulfils all wishes. Therefore it is only right to serve, cherish and hold them dear.

127. See "A Mother's Kindness" in *Teachings from the Vajrasattva Retreat*, pp. 298–300.

Amitabha Buddhist Centre, Singapore

7. Compassion is of the Utmost Need[128]

Advice to Make All Your Activities the Cause of Enlightenment

These ten powerful and inspiring quotes on compassion were compiled by Rinpoche to be used in daily prayers, as a motivation and as the basis for meditation. They are to be read and reflected upon as a reminder that compassion is of the utmost importance in our lives. Rinpoche says,

> This advice has been given so that all your activities in life will become the cause of enlightenment. Please read this especially when you have problems and relate it to those problems. This is the best psychology, the best Dharma advice and the best medicine.

COMPASSION IS OF THE UTMOST NEED

One. The Destroyer Qualified Gone Beyond One[129] said,

> The bodhisattva does not follow many Dharmas. The

---

128. These quotes were arranged and composed by Lama Zopa Rinpoche, Kopan Monastery, 11 August 2011. They were scribed by Ven. Holly Ansett and edited by Nick Ribush. They are available for free download in a beautifully designed format to be framed and displayed on the wall from Rinpoche's *Advice Page*, www.fpmt.org. The quotes have been rearranged and further edited for inclusion in this book.
129. i.e. the Buddha or "Bhagawan."

bodhisattva holds one Dharma well and realizes it well. The whole Buddhadharma will be in the hand of that person. What is that Dharma? It is great compassion.[130]

Two. What differentiates Buddhism from other religions is compassion for every single sentient being.

Three. What really pleases all the buddhas and bodhisattvas is compassion.

Four. Compassion makes all sentient beings happy.

Five. Strong compassion is the foundation that causes you to achieve full enlightenment most quickly. If you want to achieve full enlightenment in order to liberate all sentient beings from suffering and bring them to full enlightenment, the quickest way is to generate strong compassion.

Six. Chandrakirti said,[131]

> At the beginning, compassion is like a seed;
> In the middle, it is like water;
> At the end, it is like a ripened fruit.
> Achieving the result of full enlightenment is all due to
>   compassion.

Seven. Even for non-believers the best thing and only way to create merit, good karma, is compassion, as well as making offerings and prostrations to holy objects and circumambulating them,

---

130. From the Chenrezig Sutra, *Well-Condensed Dharma.*
131. *A Guide to the Middle Way*, ch.1, v.2.

even by chance. What gives all beings a happy, satisfied, meaningful and successful life is compassion.

Eight. The *Sutra Requested by Lodro Gyatso* says,

> The thought of complete enlightenment, preserving
> Dharma, practicing Dharma and having love and
> compassion for living beings: these four dharmas have
> infinite qualities—the limit of their benefits is not seen
> by the Victorious Ones.

It is saying that preserving Dharma and protecting the lives of living beings has limitless benefits. This shows that if we have compassion for sentient beings, from those we can't see with the naked eye but only under a microscope up to creatures the size of a mountain, the Buddha has never explained an end to the benefit of such compassion because it is infinite. It's the same as saving the lives of human beings, animals and insects; we must understand that it has limitless benefits.

Nine. A Kadampa geshe said,

> Holy beings of the land of Dzambu[132] respond to harm
> with good actions.

When ordinary people are harmed they retaliate with harm. Holy beings repay harm with positive actions. Whoever sees the enemy as the virtuous friend is happy wherever that person is.

The great Indian scholar bodhisattva Shantideva said in the first chapter of *A Guide to the Bodhisattva's Way of Life:*[133]

---

132. i.e. Jambudvipa (Tib. *Dzambuling*)—the name of the southern continent where we live and hence this world.
133. Ch. 1, v. 36.

I bow down to the body of him
In whom the sacred precious mind is born.
I seek refuge in that source of joy,
Who brings to happiness even those who harm him.

Ten. The extensive benefits of bodhicitta, which are like the sky and the depthless ocean, are also the benefits of generating great compassion for all sentient beings. Without great compassion there is no way to achieve bodhicitta, which has limitless benefits.

The conclusion is that compassion is the most important practice in life.

Glossary

Abhidharmakosha. *Treasury of Knowledge,* by Vasubandhu; one of the main philosophical texts studied in Tibetan monasteries.

Abhisamayalamkara. *Ornament for Clear Realizations,* by Maitreya; one of the main philosophical texts studied in Tibetan monasteries.

aggregates. The five psycho-physical constituents that make up a sentient being: form, feeling, discriminative awareness, compounding aggregates and consciousness.

Amaravati. The site of an ancient Buddhist stupa in modern Andra Pradesh, India, and also the place where Buddha first gave the Kalachakra empowerment. In 2006, His Holiness the Dalai Lama gave a Kalachakra empowerment there.

anger. One of the six root delusions; it is a disturbing thought that exaggerates the negative qualities of a person, object and so forth and then generates aversion and the wish to harm.

arhat. Literally, foe destroyer. A person who has destroyed his or her inner enemy, the delusions, and attained liberation from cyclic existence.

arura. One of the three fundamental medicines. Ordinary arura is commonly used in Tibetan medical compounds; special arura—which is said to cure any sickness—is extremely rare.

arya. Literally, noble. One who has directly realized the wisdom of emptiness.

Asanga. The fourth-century Indian master who received directly from Maitreya Buddha the extensive, or method, lineage of Shakyamuni Buddha's teachings and is said to have founded the Cittamatra School of Buddhist philosophy.

asura. Demigod. A being in the god realms who enjoys greater comfort and pleasure than human beings, but who suffers from jealousy and quarreling. See *sura.*

Atisha, Lama (982–1054). The renowned Indian master Dipamkara Shrijñana who went to Tibet in 1042 to help in the revival of Buddhism. He established the Kadam tradition and composed the *Light of the Path,* the first lam-rim text.

attachment. One of the six root delusions; a disturbing thought that exaggerates the positive aspects of a person, object and so forth and then wants to possess and not be separated from it.

bath offering practice. The practice of visualizing or actually offering an ablution to the merit field in order to clear away pollution and create merit.

beginningless rebirth. Since the continuity of the mind has no beginning, our rebirths in samsara also have no beginning.

Being Alive Again and Again. The first of the eight major hot hells.

Black Line. The second of the eight major hot hells.

bodhicitta. The altruistic determination to achieve enlightenment for the sole purpose of enlightening all sentient beings.

bodhisattva. A person whose spiritual practice is directed toward the achievement of enlightenment and who possesses the compassionate motivation of bodhicitta.

bodhisattva vows. The vows taken when one enters the bodhisattva path.

Buddha, the. The historical Buddha. See *Shakyamuni Buddha.*

Buddhadharma. The teachings of the Buddha. See *Dharma.*

Buddhahood. See *enlightenment.*

Buddhist. One who has taken refuge in the Three Jewels of Refuge: Buddha, Dharma and Sangha and who accepts the philosophical world view of the four seals: that all composite phenomena are impermanent, all contaminated phenomena are in the nature of suffering, all things and events are devoid of self-existence, and nirvana is true peace.

burning offering practice. The tantric practice of making offerings to a deity generated within a fire. Sometimes called a fire puja.

Buxa Duar. The small town in West Bengal in eastern India where the Tibetan monks who escaped to India in 1959 and wished to continue their studies were accommodated.

calm abiding. A state of concentration in which the mind is able to abide steadily without effort and for as long as desired on an object of meditation.

capable being. See *three capable beings.*

cause and effect. See *karma.*

Chakrasamvara. A male meditational deity from the mother tantra class of Highest Yoga Tantra.

Chandrakirti. The sixth century CE Indian Buddhist philosopher who wrote commentaries on Nagarjuna's philosophy. His best-known work is *A Guide to the Middle Way (Madhyamakavatara).*

Chenrezig. Avalokiteshvara, the buddha of compassion. A male meditational deity embodying fully enlightened compassion. Great Chenrezig is the form used in the two-day fasting or *nyung-nä* practice.

chöd. A tantric practice aimed at destroying self-grasping, where the practitioner visualizes dissecting and distributing the parts of the ordinary body to spirits and other beings as a feast offering.

Chöden Rinpoche (b. 1933). An ascetic, learned Gelug lama of Sera Je who meditated in a small room in Lhasa for nineteen years after the Chinese occupation; a guru of Lama Zopa Rinpoche.

cold hell. See *eight major cold hells.*

Collected Topics. The subject taught prior to debating, that lists and explains basic Buddhist terms and definitions.

college. The great Tibetan monasteries are divided into colleges, such as Sera Je and Sera Me.

circumambulation. A practice of purifying negative karma and accumulating merit in which a person walks clockwise around a holy object such as a stupa or statue.

Cittamatra. The Mind Only School, one of the four schools of Buddhist philosophy; along with Madhyamaka, one of the two Mahayana schools.

clear light. The most subtle mind. This subtlest state of mind occurs naturally at death and through successful tantric practice; it is used by practitioners to realize emptiness.

compassion. Compassion is the mind that wants to free all sentient beings from suffering; great compassion is the mind that fully accepts responsibility to do this. All sentient beings *can* be freed from their suffering because suffering depends on causes that can be removed. Therefore, in the taking and giving practice we bring to mind how sentient beings suffer helplessly in so many ways and imagine taking away all these sufferings along with their causes.

Compassion Buddha. See *Chenrezig.*

completion stage. The second of the two stages of Highest Yoga Tantra, during which control is gained over the vajra body through such practices as inner fire. It has five stages.

compounded phenomena. Phenomena that arise due to causes and conditions.

compounding aggregates. One of the five aggregates, it comprises 49 mental factors. See note 86.

contaminated aggregates. The aggregates of an ordinary being that are contaminated by the seed of delusion and therefore pervaded by suffering because they are controlled by delusion and karma.

conventional truth. As opposed to ultimate truth, which is the understanding of the ultimate nature of reality (emptiness), conventional truth is what is true to the valid conventional consciousness. Rinpoche translates it as "truth for the all-obscuring mind" because although it is true, it obscures the ultimate nature. Conventional and ultimate truth form the important subject in Buddhist philosophy called the two truths.

cyclic existence. See *samsara.*

daka. Literally, a sky-goer. A male being who helps arouse blissful energy in a qualified tantric practitioner.

dakini. Literally, a female sky-goer. A female being who helps arouse blissful energy in a qualified tantric practitioner.

definitive meaning. As opposed to the interpretative meaning, it is the meaning that is no longer open to interpretation.

deity. An emanation of the enlightened mind used as the object of meditation in tantric practices.

delusion. An obscuration covering the essentially pure nature of the mind causing suffering and dissatisfaction; the main delusion is ignorance and all the others come from this. See *three poisonous minds, root delusions* and *twenty secondary delusions.*

dependent origination. Also called dependent arising. The way that the self and phenomena exist conventionally as relative and interdependent. They come into existence in dependence upon (1) causes and conditions, (2) their parts and, most subtly, (3) the mind imputing, or labeling, them. See *twelve dependent related limbs.*

desire realm. One of the three realms of samsara, comprising the hell beings, hungry ghosts, animals, humans, asuras and the six lower classes of suras; beings in this realm are preoccupied with desire for objects of the six senses.

deva. A god dwelling in a state with much comfort and pleasure in the desire, form or formless realms.

Dharamsala. A village in the north-west of India, in Himachal Pradesh. It is the residence of His Holiness the Dalai Lama and the Tibetan Government-in-Exile.

Dharma. The second refuge jewel. Literally, "that which holds or protects (us from suffering)" and hence brings happiness and leads us toward liberation and enlightenment. In Buddhism, absolute Dharma is the realizations attained along the path to liberation and enlightenment and conventional Dharma is seen as both the teachings of the Buddha and virtuous actions.

Dharma protectors. Beings, some worldly and others enlightened, who protect Dharma teachings and practitioners.

dharmakaya. The truth, or wisdom, body of a buddha (the other body being the form body, or *rupakaya*); the blissful omniscient mind of a buddha, the result of the wisdom side of the path. It can be divided into the natural truth body and the emptiness truth body. See also *three kayas.*

Drepung Monastery. The largest of the three major Gelug monasteries. It was founded near Lhasa by one of Lama Tsongkhapa's disciples and is now re-established in exile in south India. The two main colleges are Loseling and Gomang.

Dromtönpa (1005–64). Lama Atisha's heart disciple and chief translator in Tibet; propagator of the Kadampa tradition. He is said to be a previous emanation of His Holiness the Dalai Lama.

Denma Lochö Rinpoche (b. 1928). An outstanding scholar and master of Drepung Loseling and ex-abbot of Namgyal Monastery. He is one of Lama Zopa Rinpoche's gurus.

effortful bodhicitta. A bodhicitta that is not effortless and spontaneous but contrived. See *bodhicitta.*

eight auspicious symbols. Or eight symbols of good fortune. They are the right-turning conch, glorious endless knot, golden fishes, lotus, parasol, treasure vase, wheel and victory banner. See *Buddhist Symbols*, pp. 17–38.

eight freedoms. The eight states from which a perfect human rebirth is free: being born as a hell-being, hungry ghost, animal, long-life god or barbarian or in a dark age when no buddha has descended; holding wrong views; and being born with defective mental or physical faculties.

eight Mahayana precepts. A set of vows taken for one day with the bodhicitta motivation to abandon killing, stealing, lying, sexual contact, intoxicants, high seats, eating at the wrong time, singing and dancing, and wearing perfumes and jewelry.

eight major hot hells. The hell of Being Alive Again and Again, the Black Line Hell, the Gathered and Crushed Hell, the Hell of Crying, the Hell of Great Crying, the Hot Hell, the Extremely Hot Hell and the Inexhaustible Hot Hell.

eight major cold hells. The Hell of Blisters, the Hell of Bursting Blisters, the Hell of A-choo, the Moaning Hell, the Clenched-teeth Hell, the Hell of Cracking Like an Utpala Flower, the Hell of Cracking Like a Lotus, and the Hell of Great Cracking Like a Lotus.

eight substances. The mirror, *ghiwang* medicine, yoghurt, long life (*durva*) grass, *bilva* fruit, right-turning conch, cinnabar and mustard seeds. See *Buddhist Symbols,* pp. 41–63.

eight sufferings of humans. Birth, old age, sickness, death, worry and fear about meeting what you don't want, not being able to find what you do want, not getting any satisfaction when you do find what you want and the pervasive compounding suffering of the aggregates.

eight worldly dharmas. The worldly concerns that generally motivate the actions of ordinary beings: being happy when given gifts and unhappy when not given them; wanting to be happy and not wanting to be unhappy; wanting praise and not wanting criticism; wanting a good reputation and not wanting a bad reputation.

eighteen qualities of a perfect human rebirth. See *eight freedoms* and *ten richnesses.*

emptiness (Skt: *shunyata*). The absence of all false ideas about how things exist. Specifically, it refers to the lack of the apparent independent, self-existence of phenomena.

enlightenment. Full awakening, or buddhahood. It is the ultimate goal of Buddhist practice, attained when all limitations have been removed from the mind and one's positive potential has been completely and perfectly realized. It is a state characterized by infinite compassion, wisdom and skill.

eon. A world period, an inconceivably long period of time. The life span of the universe is divided into four great eons which are themselves divided into twenty lesser eons.

exchanging self for others. The second of two methods used in Tibetan Buddhism to develop bodhicitta, the other being the sevenfold cause and effect instruction. It has five steps: equalizing oneself with others, the disadvantages of cherishing the self, the advantages of cherishing others, exchanging self for others and taking and giving.

equanimity. Absence of the usual discrimination of sentient beings into friend, enemy and stranger, deriving from the realization that all sentient beings are equal in wanting happiness and not wanting suffering and that since beginningless time, all beings have been all things to each other. It is an impartial mind that serves as the basis for the development of great love, great compassion and bodhicitta.

five great Sakya pandits. The five great masters (patriarchs) who founded the Sakya tradition: Sachen Küngya Nyingpo (1092–1158), Lobpön Sonam Tsemo (1142–82), Jetsün Drakpa Gyaltsen (1147–1216), Sakya Pandita (1182–1251) and Drogön Chögyal Phagpa (1235–80).

five great treatises. The five main texts studied in the great Gelug monasteries: the Abhisamayalamkara, Vinaya, Madhyamaka, Abhidharmakosha and Pramanavarttika.

five lay vows. The precepts taken by lay Buddhist practitioners for life, to abstain from killing, stealing, lying, sexual misconduct and taking intoxicants.

five major sutra texts. See *five great treatises.*

five negative karmas without break. Also called the five uninterrupted negative karmas, these are five actions so heavy that they cause one to be reborn in hell in the next life without the break of another rebirth in-between. They are killing one's mother, killing one's father, killing an arhat, maliciously drawing blood from a buddha and creating a schism in the Sangha.

five paths. There are five paths to liberation and five paths to enlightenment. The names are the same but they differ due to the motivation of the practitioner. They are the path of merit, the preparatory path, right-seeing path, path of meditation and path of no more learning.

five powers. These are five forces to be *integrated into the whole lifetime* and five to be *practiced near the time of death.* See notes 44 and 45.

five precepts. See *five lay vows.*

five signs of nearing death of suras. The five sufferings experienced by desire realm gods at the time of death: their bodies become unattractive, their throne is no longer comfortable, their flower garlands wilt, their clothes stain and their bodies smell.

form realm. The second of samsara's three realms, with seventeen classes of gods.

formless realm. The highest of samsara's three realms, with four classes of gods involved in formless meditations.

four classes of tantra. The division of tantra into *Kriya* (Action), *Charya* (Performance), *Yoga* and *Anuttara Yoga Tantra* (Highest Yoga Tantra, also sometimes *Maha-anuttara Yoga Tantra*).

four parts of an action. The four things needed to make an action of body or speech complete so that the full result is experienced. They are the intention, object, action and completion. Each of these four brings its own result and—if it is negative—can be purified by one of the four opponent powers. Actions that lack all four parts are weaker in strength and bring weaker results.

four noble truths. The subject of the Buddha's first turning of the Wheel of Dharma: the truths of suffering, the origin of suffering, the cessation of suffering and the path to the cessation of suffering as seen by an arya being.

four opponent powers. The four practices used to purify non-virtuous imprints on the mind stream. They are the power of the object, taking refuge in the Triple Gem and generating bodhicitta; the power of regret, feeling deep regret for the negativity committed; the power of resolve, determining not to repeat that negativity; and the power of remedy, a practice such as Vajrasattva or the Thirty-five Buddhas that effectively acts as an antidote to the negativity.

four traditions in Tibet. The four major schools of Tibetan Buddhism: Nyingma, Kagyü, Sakya and Gelug.

four vital points of analysis. One of the main techniques for meditating on emptiness. See note 90.

Ganden Monastery. The first of the three great Gelug monastic universities near Lhasa, founded in 1409 by Lama Tsongkhapa. It was badly damaged in the 1960s and has now been re-established in exile in South India. Its two main colleges are Jangtse and Shartse.

Ganden Tripa. "Holder of the Throne of Ganden," Lama Tsongkhapa's representative, head of the Gelug tradition.

Gelek Rimpoche (b. 1939). A Gelug lama and lharampa geshe from Drepung Monastery born in Tibet and a friend of Lama Yeshe and Lama Zopa Rinpoche. He is the founder and president of the Jewel Heart organization of Dharma centers.

gelong. A fully ordained Buddhist monk.

Gelug. Literally, the "Virtuous Order." The order of Tibetan Buddhism founded by Lama Tsongkhapa and his disciples in the early fifteenth century and the most recent of the four main schools of Tibetan Buddhism. It was developed from the Kadam School founded by Atisha and Dromtönpa.

generation stage. The first of the two stages of Highest Yoga Tantra, during which one cultivates the clear appearance and divine pride of one's chosen meditational deity.

geshe. Literally, a "spiritual friend." The title conferred on those who have completed extensive studies and examinations at Gelug monastic universities. The highest level of geshe is the *lharampa.*

graduated path or *lam-rim.* A presentation of Shakyamuni Buddha's teachings in a form suitable for the step-by-step training of a disciple. The lam-rim was first formulated by the great Indian teacher Lama Atisha when he came to Tibet in 1042. It presents the practice in three levels suited to the three capable beings.

Great Chenrezig. See *Chenrezig.*

great liberation. A synonym for enlightenment.

Great Treatise on the Stages of the Path to Enlightenment, The (Lam-rim Chen-mo). One of Lama Tsongkhapa's most important works and a fundamental lam-rim text; a commentary to Lama Atisha's *Light of the Path.*

grounds. There are ten grounds, or *bhumi,* on the bodhisattva path to full enlightenment.

guru or *lama.* Spiritual guide. One who shows a disciple the path to liberation and enlightenment. Literally, "heavy" with knowledge of the Dharma. In tantra, the guru is seen as inseparable from the meditational deity and the Three Jewels of Refuge. See also *root guru.*

guru-deity. The inseparability of the deity and spiritual master, a fundamental practice of tantra.

guru devotion. The sutra or tantric practice of seeing the guru as a buddha then devoting to him or her with thought and with action.

guru yoga. The fundamental tantric practice, whereby one's guru is seen as identical with the buddhas, one's personal meditational deity and the essential nature of one's own mind.

Guru Puja (Tib: *Lama Chöpa).* A special Highest Yoga Tantra guru yoga practice composed by Panchen Losang Chökyi Gyaltsen.

Guru Shakyamuni Buddha. See Shakyamuni Buddha.

Heart Sutra. A short *Perfection of Wisdom Sutra* that is commonly recited at the monasteries before teachings and debate.

hell. The samsaric realm with the greatest suffering. There are eight major hot hells, eight major cold hells and four neighboring hells.

higher capable being. The highest of the three levels of practice. The higher capable being has the goal of full enlightenment. See also *lower* and *middle capable being.*

higher realms. The higher realms comprise the more fortunate rebirths as a human, sura or asura.

Highest Yoga Tantra. The fourth and supreme division of tantric practice, sometimes called *Maha-Anuttara Yoga Tantra.* It consists of the generation and completion stages. Through this practice one can attain full enlightenment within one lifetime.

hot hell. See *eight major hot hells.*

house. In Tibetan monasteries colleges are divided into houses (*khangtsen*), and monks are generally assigned to these houses according to the region of Tibet (or neighboring countries) from which they come.

Hundred Devas of Tushita. The first words and hence the title of the *Guru Yoga of Lama Tsongkhapa, Ganden Lha Gyäma.*

hungry ghost or *preta.* A kind of ghost, or spirit. One of the three lower realms of cyclic existence.

ignorance. Literally, "not seeing" that which exists or the way in which things exist. There are basically two kinds of ignorance: ignorance of karma and ignorance of ultimate truth. Ignorance is the fundamental delusion from which all others spring. It is the first of the twelve dependent related limbs.

impermanence. The gross and subtle levels of the transience of phenomena. The moment things and events come into existence, their disintegration has already begun.

incarnate lama. A tulku or reincarnated lama, is someone who through the mind of bodhicitta can choose where to be reborn in order to best serve all sentient beings.

initiation. Transmission received from a tantric master allowing a disciple to engage in the practices of a particular meditational deity. It is also referred to as an empowerment.

inner offering. A tantric offering whose basis of transformation is one's five aggregates visualized as the five meats and five nectars.

interferers. Various hindering spirits who try to prevent pure Dharma practice.

intermediate state. The state between death and rebirth.

interpretive meaning. The interpretive meaning, as opposed to the definitive meaning, is that which is still open to interpretation.

Jinpa, Geshe Thupten (b. 1959). A respected author, Cambridge graduate and principal translator of His Holiness the Dalai Lama.

Kadampa geshe. A practitioner of the Kadam lineage founded in the eleventh century by Atisha, Dromtönpa and their followers. Kadampa geshes are renowned for their practice of thought transformation. They are the forerunners of the Gelug School.

Kadampa teachings. The teachings of the Kadam lineage.

Kagyü. The order of Tibetan Buddhism founded in the eleventh century by Marpa, Milarepa, Gampopa, and their followers. It is one of the four main schools of Tibetan Buddhism.

Kalachakra. Literally, "Cycle of Time." A male meditational deity of Highest Yoga Tantra. The *Kalachakra Tantra* contains instructions on medicine, astronomy and so forth.

Kangyur. The part of the Tibetan Canon that contains the sutras and tantras; literally, "translation of the (Buddha's) word." It contains 108 volumes.

karma. Action; the process of cause and effect, whereby positive (virtuous) actions produce happiness and negative (non-virtuous) actions produce suffering.

karmic view. The way in which things appear to us influenced by karma created in the past.

kaya. A buddha-body, or holy body; the body of an enlightened being. See also *three kayas.*

Khunu Lama Tenzin Gyaltsen (1895–1977). An Indian scholar of Sanskrit and Tibetan and a great master and teacher of the Rime (nonsectarian) tradition of Tibetan Buddhism. He famously gave teachings to His Holiness the Dalai Lama on Shantideva's *Guide* and was also a guru of Lama Zopa Rinpoche. He composed a famous text, *The Jewel Lamp: A Praise of Bodhicitta*, translated into English as *Vast as the Heavens, Deep as the Sea.*

Kriya Tantra. The first of four classes of tantra, also called Action Tantra, because it emphasizes external activities, such as prayers, mudras and so forth.

lam-rim. See *graduated path.*

Lamrimpa, Geshe (1922–97?). Ngawang Phuntsog, a highly learned lama from Drepung Monastery who remained in Tibet and did not go into exile.

Lama Tsongkhapa. See *Tsongkhapa.*

Lawudo. The cave in the Solu Khumbu region of Nepal where the Lawudo Lama meditated for more than twenty years. Lama Zopa Rinpoche is recognized as the reincarnation of the Lawudo Lama.

lay vows. See *Pratimoksha* and *five lay vows*

Lesser Vehicle. The Hinayana or "Lesser Vehicle" is one of the two general divisions of Buddhism. Lesser Vehicle practitioners' motivation for following the Dharma path is principally their intense wish for personal liberation from conditioned existence, or samsara. Two types of Lesser Vehicle practitioner are identified: Hearers and Solitary Realizers.

lharampa geshe. See *geshe.*

liberation. The state of complete freedom from samsara which is the goal of a Lesser Vehicle practitioner seeking his or her own escape from suffering. "Lower nirvana" is used to refer to this state of self-liberation, while "great nirvana" or "great liberation" refers to the supreme attainment of the full enlightenment of buddhahood.

Ling Rinpoche (1903–83). An outstanding Gelug master from Drepung Monastery, senior tutor to His Holiness the Fourteenth Dalai Lama and 97th Ganden Tripa, he was also a guru of Lama Yeshe and Lama Zopa Rinpoche. The current incarnation is studying in south India.

lo-jong. See *mind training.*

Longchen Rabjampa (1308–64). A great Buddhist teacher and master of the Nyingma tradition who composed many major texts and practices.

loving kindness. Loving kindness is the mind that wants all sentient beings to experience all happiness, not just temporary samsaric pleasure but particularly the ultimate happiness of liberation and enlightenment. Great loving kindness is the mind that takes on the responsibility to do this. All sentient beings can experience all happiness because happiness depends on causes. Therefore, in the taking and giving practice we sincerely dedicate all our own causes for happiness and the results these would bring along with all our actual present happiness to all sentient beings and think they receive them.

lower nirvana. See *liberation.*

lower realms. The three realms of cyclic existence with the most suffering: the hell, hungry ghost and animal realms.

Lower Tantric College. One of the five major learning monasteries of the Gelug school; it was founded in 1433 by Je Sherab Senge, a disciple of Lama Tsongkhapa.

lower capable being. The first of the three levels of practice of the lamrim, the lower capable being has the goal of a better future existence. See also *middle, higher* and *three capable beings.*

Madhyamaka. The Middle Way School of Buddhist philosophy; a system of analysis founded by Nagarjuna based on the *Perfection of Wisdom Sutras* of Shakyamuni Buddha and considered to be the supreme presentation of the wisdom of emptiness. This view holds that all phenomena are dependent originations and thereby avoids the mistaken extremes of self-existence and non-existence, or eternalism and nihilism. It has two divisions, Svatantrika and Prasangika. Along with Cittamatra, it is one of the two Mahayana schools of philosophy.

Madhyamakavatara. A famous text composed by Chandrakirti to supplement Nagarjuna's treatise *Mulamadhyamakakarika.* It is used as the main sourcebook by most Tibetan monasteries for the study of emptiness.

Madhyamaka Prasangika School. See *Prasangika.*

Mahayana. The "Great Vehicle"; one of the two general divisions of Buddhism. Mahayana practitioners' motivation for following the

Dharma path is principally their intense wish for all mother sentient beings to be liberated from conditioned existence, or samsara, and to attain the full enlightenment of buddhahood. The Mahayana has two divisions, Mahayana Paramitayana (Sutrayana) and Mahayana Tantrayana (Vajrayana or Mantrayana). See also *Lesser Vehicle*.

Maitreya Buddha. After Shakyamuni Buddha, the next (and fifth) of the thousand buddhas of this fortunate eon to descend to turn the wheel of Dharma. Presently residing in the pure land of Tushita (Ganden). Recipient of the method lineage of Shakyamuni Buddha's teachings, which, in a mystical transmission, he passed on to Asanga.

mandala. A circular diagram symbolic of the entire universe. The abode of a meditational deity.

mantra. Literally, "mind protection." Mantras are Sanskrit syllables— usually recited in conjunction with the practice of a particular meditational deity—and embody the qualities of the deity with which they are associated.

Marpa (1012–96). The founder of the Kagyü tradition of Tibetan Buddhism; he was a renowned tantric master and translator, a disciple of Naropa and the guru of Milarepa.

Maudgalyayana. One of Buddha's two closest disciples, along with Shariputra; he was considered the disciple most accomplished in miraculous powers developed through meditation.

merely labeled I. This is the valid I, the way in which the I actually exists.

merit. Positive imprints left on the mind by virtuous, or Dharma, actions. They are the main cause of experiencing happiness. Accumulation of merit, when coupled with the accumulation of wisdom, eventually results in the form body of a buddha.

middle capable being. The second of the three levels of practice, or scopes, the middle capable being has the goal of liberation from suffering. See also *lower* and *higher capable being*.

merit field. Visualized or actual holy beings who are the field of accumulation of merit by performing practices such as going for refuge, making offerings and so forth and to whom one prays or makes requests for special purposes.

Milarepa (1040–1123). One of Tibet's greatest yogis, he achieved enlightenment in one lifetime under the tutelage of his guru, Marpa. One of the founding fathers of the Kagyü School.

mind. Synonymous with consciousness and sentience. Defined as that which is "clear and knowing"; a formless entity that has the ability to perceive objects. Mind is divided into six primary consciousnesses and fifty-one mental factors.

mind training. The powerful *lo-jong,* or thought training, approach to the development of bodhicitta in which the mind is trained to use all situations, both happy and unhappy, as a means of destroying self-cherishing and self-grasping.

Mt. Meru. The center of the universe in Buddhist cosmology.

Nagarjuna. The great second-century Indian philosopher and tantric adept who propounded the Madhyamaka philosophy of emptiness.

negative action. See *nonvirtue.*

neighboring hells. Four hells surrounding the major hot hells; they are the Fiery Trench, Putrid Swamp, Uncrossable Torrent and Plain of Knives.

nirmanakaya. The buddha body of perfect emanation, in which a fully enlightened being appears in order to benefit ordinary beings. See also *three kayas.*

nirvana. See *liberation.*

nonvirtue. Negative karma; any action that results in suffering.

Nyingma. The old translation school of Tibetan Buddhism, which traces its teachings back to the time of Padmasambhava, the eighth century Indian tantric master invited to Tibet by King Trisong Detsen to clear away hindrances to the establishment of Buddhism in Tibet. It is the first of the four main schools of Tibetan Buddhism.

nyung-nä. A two-day Thousand-arm Chenrezig retreat that involves fasting, prostrations and silence.

object to be refuted. The appearance of inherent existence; it is conceived by an awareness conceiving true existence.

OM MANI PADME HUM. The mantra of Chenrezig, Buddha of compassion.

omniscience. See *enlightenment.*

Pabongka Dechen Nyingpo (1871–1941). An influential and charismatic lama of the Gelug School who was the root guru of His Holiness the Dalai Lama's senior and junior tutors. He gave a famous set of teachings which were later compiled by His Holiness Trijang Rinpoche into *Liberation in the Palm of Your Hand.*

Padmasambhava. The eighth-century Indian tantric master mainly responsible for the establishment of Buddhism in Tibet. He is revered by all Tibetan Buddhists, especially Nyingmapas.

path. See *five paths.*

perfect human rebirth. The rare human state that has all the conditions for practicing Dharma and attaining enlightenment. It possesses eighteen special qualities. See *eight freedoms* and *ten richnesses.*

Perfection of Wisdom Sutras (*Prajñaparamita*). The teachings of Shakyamuni Buddha in which the wisdom of emptiness and the path of the bodhisattva are set forth. The basis of Nagarjuna's philosophy.

pervasive compounding suffering. The fact that the samsaric aggregates are pervaded by suffering being under the control of delusions and karma. See note 57.

Potowa, Geshe (1031–1105). Also known as Potowa Rinchen Sel. He entered Reting Monastery in 1058 and became its abbot for a short time. He was one of the three great disciples of Dromtönpa, patriarch of the Kadampa Treatise lineage.

Pramanavarttika. Dharmakirti's *Commentary on Dignaga's Compendium of Valid Cognition, (Pramanasamuccaya)*; one of five major treatises studied in the Tibetan monasteries.

Prasangika. The Middle Way Autonomy School of the four schools of Buddhist philosophy. See also *Madhyamaka.*

pratimoksha vows. Eight different levels of vows for individual liberation; five sets are for monastics and three are for lay people, including the five lay vows and the one day vows.

preliminary practices. Practices that prepare the mind for successful tantric meditation by removing hindrances and accumulating merit.

preta. See *hungry ghost.*

puja. Literally, "offering"; a religious ceremony. Puja is usually used to describe an offering ceremony such as the *Guru Puja,* which is a devotional offering practice to the spiritual guide in which one both purifies negativity and accumulates merit.

pure land. A pure land of a buddha is a place where there is no suffering. In some but not all pure lands, after taking birth, the practitioner receives teachings directly from the buddha of that pure land, actualizes the rest of the path and then becomes enlightened.

purification. The eradication from the mind of negative imprints left by past non-virtuous actions that would otherwise ripen into suffering. The most effective methods of purification employ the four opponent powers of regret, reliance, virtuous activity and resolve.

Rabten Rinpoche, Geshe (1920–86). A learned Gelug lama who was a religious assistant to His Holiness the Dalai Lama before moving to Switzerland in 1975 and a guru of Lama Yeshe and Lama Zopa Rinpoche.

Rachevsky, Zina (1931–73). Lama Yeshe's and Lama Zopa Rinpoche's first Western student. She helped them establish Kopan Monastery and died in retreat in Solu Khumbu.

Rajgir. The ancient capital of the Magadha kingdom located in modern Bihar. It is close to Vulture's Peak, where the Buddha taught the *Perfection of Wisdom Sutras* when turning the middle Wheel of Dharma.

real I. The I that appears to exist from its own side without depending on anything—such as causes and conditions, parts or the mind's imputation. It is the object to be refuted.

red distribution. See *chöd.*

renunciation. A heartfelt feeling of complete disgust with cyclic existence such that day and night one yearns for liberation and engages in the practices that secure it. It is the first of the three principal aspects of the path to enlightenment.

Ribur Rinpoche (1923–2006). A great lama from Sera Me who was recognized as a reincarnation by the Thirteenth Dalai Lama. He suffered under Chinese oppression for twenty-one years but later traveled to and taught in many countries and settled in the USA. He was a guru of Lama Zopa Rinpoche.

right view. See *emptiness.*

rinpoche. Literally, "precious one." An epithet for an incarnate lama who has intentionally taken rebirth in a human form to benefit sentient beings on the path to enlightenment, it is also given as a title to great teachers and practitioners. See also *tulku.*

root delusions. The six root delusions are anger, attachment, pride, ignorance, doubt and deluded views.

root guru. The teacher who has had the greatest influence upon a particular disciple's entering or following the spiritual path.

Sadaprarudita. The ever-weeping bodhisattva; he is mentioned in the *Perfection of Wisdom Sutras* and used as an example of unwavering devotion to the guru.

sadhana. Method of accomplishment; the step-by-step instructions for practicing the meditations related to a particular meditational deity.

Sakya. One of the four main schools of Tibetan Buddhism. It was founded in the eleventh century in the south of the province of Tsang by Khön Konchog Gyälpo (1034–1102).

sambhogakaya. The buddha-body of perfect resource, or enjoyment body; the form in which the enlightened mind appears in order to benefit highly realized bodhisattvas. See also *three kayas.*

samsara. The beginningless, recurring cycle of death and rebirth into the six realms of existence under the control of delusion and karma, fraught with suffering. It can also refer to the contaminated aggregates of a sentient being.

Sangha. The spiritual community; the third of the Three Jewels of Refuge. The absolute Sangha are those who have directly realized emptiness; the relative Sangha are ordained monks and nuns.

Saraha. A great eighth century Indian yogi; one of the eighty-four *mahasiddhas* and founders of the Vajrayana, particularly the *mahamudra* tradition. He composed many famous tantric songs.

Sarnath. Located near Varanasi in modern Bihar, it is the site of the Deer Park, where the Buddha taught the four noble truths in the first turning of the Wheel of Dharma.

self-cherishing. An excessive concern with one's own happiness at the expense of others. It is the main obstacle to achieving bodhicitta.

sentient being. Any unenlightened being; any being whose mind is not completely free from gross and subtle ignorance.

Sera Monastery. One of the three great Gelug monasteries near Lhasa. It was founded in the early fifteenth century by Jamchen Chöje, a disciple of Lama Tsongkhapa, and is now also established in exile in south India. It has two colleges, Sera Je, with which Lama Zopa Rinpoche is connected, and Sera Me.

Serkong Rinpoche, Tsenshab (1914–83). A great scholar and yogi chosen as "debating partner" for His Holiness the Dalai Lama in Tibet who later became one of His Holiness's gurus in India. He was an incarnation of Marpa Lotsawa's son Darma Dode. A close teacher of Lama Zopa Rinpoche, he encouraged Rinpoche to spread the practice of the Chenrezig fasting retreat in the world. The current incarnation lives in Dharamsala.

seven perfect royal objects. The seven possessions of a universal emperor: the wheel, jewel, queen, minister, elephant, horse and general. See *Buddhist Symbols*, pp. 65–85.

seven treasures of arya beings. Faith, ethics, study, generosity, shame, conscientiousness and wisdom.

Shakyamuni Buddha (563–483 BC). The fourth of the thousand founding buddhas of this present world age. Born a prince of the Shakya clan in northern India, he achieved enlightenment in Bodhgaya and gradually revealed the sutra and tantra paths to liberation and enlightenment, becoming the founder of what is now known as Buddhism.

Shantideva. The great eighth-century Indian Buddhist philosopher and bodhisattva who composed the essential Mahayana text, *A Guide to the Bodhisattva's Way of Life.*

Shariputra. One of the two principal disciples of the Buddha, the other being Maudgalyayana.

shem-thab. The lower part of a Tibetan monk's or nun's robes.

shunyata. See emptiness.

Six Ornaments. The great scholars Nagarjuna, Aryadeva, Asanga, Vasubandhu, Dharmakirti and Dignaga.

six perfections. The six practices of a bodhisattva: the perfections of generosity, morality, patience, enthusiastic perseverance, concentration and wisdom.

six realms. The three suffering realms (hell, hungry ghost and animal) and three fortunate realms (human, sura and asura) of cyclic existence.

six root delusions. See *root delusions.*

Six Yogas of Naropa. A set of completion stage tantric practices that comprise the inner fire meditation, the yoga of the illusory body, the yoga of clear light, transference of consciousness, transference into another body and the yoga of the intermediate state.

Sopa Rinpoche, Geshe (b. 1923). An eminent Buddhist scholar based at Deer Park, Wisconsin, USA, and a guru of Lama Yeshe and Lama Zopa Rinpoche.

sleeping yoga with creativity, or *mental fabrication.* A Highest Yoga Tantra practice where the practitioner goes to sleep visualized as the guru-deity in the mandala and so forth.

sleeping yoga without creativity, or *mental fabrication.* A Highest Yoga Tantra practice where the practitioner uses sleep to meditate on emptiness or the *dharmakaya.*

Song Rinpoche (1905–1984). A powerful Gelug lama renowned for his wrathful aspect who had impeccable knowledge of Tibetan Buddhist rituals, art and science. He was one of Lama Yeshe's and Lama Zopa Rinpoche's principal tantric gurus. The present incarnation is currently studying in south India.

Sravasti. The ancient kingdom of the Kosalas now situated in modern Uttar Pradesh. It is the site of the Jeta Grove, where Buddha would spend the rainy season in retreat and many ruins from that time have been excavated.

stages of the path to enlightenment. See *lam-rim.*

subtle defilement. The subtle obscurations of the mind that obstruct the attainment of enlightenment.

Sudhana. The main character in the *Gandavyuha Sutra,* the last chapter of the *Avatamsaka (Flower Ornament) Sutra.* Sudhana is a youth whose search for enlightenment takes him on a journey to fifty-three spiritual teachers; he is used as an example of perfect guru devotion.

suffering of change. Experiences that are normally regarded as pleasure but which are in reality only suffering.

suffering of pain. The commonly recognized suffering experiences of pain, discomfort and unhappiness.

sura. Another term for a deva, or god.

sutra. A discourse of Buddha; the pre-tantric division of Buddhist teachings stressing the cultivation of bodhicitta and the practice of the six perfections. See also *Mahayana Paramitayana.*

taking and giving or *tong-len.* The meditation practice of generating bodhicitta by taking on the suffering of others and giving them happiness. See also *compassion, exchanging self for others* and *loving kindness.*

tantra. Literally, "thread," or "continuity." The secret teachings of the Buddha; a scriptural text and the teachings and practices it contains. Also called Tantrayana, Vajrayana or Mantrayana.

tantric vows. Vows taken by tantric practitioners.

Tashi Lhunpo Monastery. The Panchen Lama's monastery in Shigatse, Tibet. It was built by the First Dalai Lama, Gyalwa Gendun Drub, and contains one temple devoted to a large Maitreya Buddha statue.

Tara. A female meditational deity who embodies the enlightened activity of all the buddhas; often referred to as the mother of the buddhas of the past, present and future. The *Twenty-one Praises to Tara* prayer is usually recited before debate sessions at the monasteries.

tathagata. Literally, "one who has realized suchness," meaning a buddha.

Tehor Khampa monks. Monks from the Tehor region in the eastern part of Kham in Tibet.

temporary happiness. The worldly happiness of humans and gods.

ten grounds or *bhumi.* The ten stages traversed by a bodhisattva on the way to enlightenment.

ten richnesses. The ten qualities that characterize a perfect human rebirth: being born as a human being; in a Dharma country; and with perfect mental and physical faculties; being free from the five uninterrupted negative karmas; having faith in Buddha's teachings; being born when a buddha has descended; the continued existence of the Buddha's teaching; the existence of living, experienced teachings; when there are still followers of the teachings; and having the necessary conditions to practice Dharma. See *perfect human rebirth.*

Tengyur. The part of the Tibetan Canon that contains the Indian pandits' commentaries on the Buddha's teachings. Literally, "translation of the commentaries." It contains about 225 volumes (depending on the edition).

Theravada Buddhism. One of the eighteen schools into which the Lesser Vehicle split not long after Shakyamuni Buddha's death; it is the dominant Lesser Vehicle School today, prevalent in Thailand, Sri Lanka and Burma and well represented in the West.

Thirty-five Buddhas. Also called the "Thirty-five Buddhas of Confession"; a powerful practice for confessing and purifying negative karmas. These thirty-five buddhas are visualized as the merit field while reciting *The Sutra of the Three Heaps* and performing prostrations.

thirty-seven aids to enlightenment. Also called the thirty-seven wings of, or harmonies of, enlightenment. (1) The four close placements of mindfulness; (2) the four thorough abandonments; (3) the four legs of magical manifestation; (4) the five powers; (5) the five strengths; (6) the seven branches of enlightenment; and (7) the eight branches of superiors' path.

three capable beings. Three different levels of practice based on the motivations of trying to attain a better future rebirth, liberation or enlightenment. See *lower, middle* and *higher capable being.*

three higher trainings. Ethics, concentration and wisdom.

three kayas. The dharmakaya (wisdom body), sambhogakaya (enjoyment body) and nirmanakaya (emanation body). The general way a buddha is described as emanating after enlightenment, the wisdom body being a result of the wisdom side of the practice and the form bodies of the sambhogakaya and nirmanakaya being a result of the method side. See also *dharmakaya, nirmanakaya, sambhogakaya.*

three levels of vows. The pratimoksha, bodhicitta and tantric vows.

three poisonous minds. The three root delusions of anger, attachment and ignorance.

three principal aspects of the path. The three main divisions of the lam-rim: renunciation, bodhicitta and the right view (of emptiness).

three types of suffering. All the suffering of samsara can be grouped into these three: the suffering of suffering, the suffering of change and pervasive compounding suffering.

Trijang Rinpoche (1900–81). A famous Gelug master and junior tutor to His Holiness the Dalai Lama; a direct disciple of Pabongka Rinpoche who edited *Liberation in the Palm of Your Hand.* He was the root guru of many Gelug lamas including Lama Yeshe and Lama Zopa Rinpoche.

truly existent. The way things appear to exist from their own side without depending on causes and conditions, parts or the mind's imputation. It is the object to be refuted.

truth for the all-obscuring mind. See *conventional truth.*

tsog. Literally a "gathering"; a gathering of offering substances and a gathering of disciples to make the offerings.

Tsongkhapa, Lama (1357–1417). The founder of the Gelug tradition of Tibetan Buddhism; he revitalized many sutra and tantra lineages and the monastic tradition in Tibet.

tulku. See *incarnate lama.*

Tushita Pure Land. The "Joyous Land" (Ganden). The pure land of the thousand buddhas of this eon, where the future buddha Maitreya and Lama Tsongkhapa reside.

twelve deeds of the Buddha. The twelve deeds that Guru Shakyamuni Buddha and all buddhas perform: descending from Tushita Heaven, entering his mother's womb, birth, studying arts and handicrafts, enjoying life in the palace, renunciation, undertaking ascetic practices, going to Bodhgaya, defeating the negative forces (Mara), attaining enlightenment, turning the wheel of Dharma and entering parinirvana.

twelve dependent related limbs. Also called the twelve links of dependent origination; the twelve steps in the evolution of cyclic existence: ignorance, karmic formation, consciousness, name and form, sensory fields, contact, feelings, attachment, grasping, becoming (existence), birth and aging and death. This is Shakyamuni Buddha's explanation of how delusion and karma bind sentient beings to samsara, causing them to be reborn into suffering again and again; depicted pictorially in the Tibetan "Wheel of Life."

twenty secondary delusions. Belligerence, resentment, concealment, spite, jealousy, miserliness, deceit, dissimulation, haughtiness, harmfulness, non-shame, non-embarrassment, lethargy, excitement, non-faith, laziness, non-conscientiousness, forgetfulness, non-introspection and distraction. See also *delusion*.

ultimate happiness. Liberation and enlightenment.

ultimate truth. One of the two truths, the other being conventional truth or "truth for the all obscuring mind." It is the understanding of the ultimate nature of things and events, i.e. their emptiness.

Vaishali. The ancient capital of the Licchavis, located in modern Bihar. Buddha visited the city many times and it was here that he turned the final Wheel of Dharma.

Vajrasattva. A male meditational deity symbolizing the inherent purity of all the buddhas. Reciting his mantra is a major tantric purification practice for removing obstacles created by negative karma and the breaking of vows.

Vajradhara. A male meditational deity and the form in which Shakyamuni Buddha revealed the teachings of secret mantra. The "unified state of Vajradhara" is a synonym for enlightenment.

Vinaya. The Buddha's teachings on ethical discipline (morality), monastic conduct and so forth; along with the Abhidharma and the Sutra, one of the three baskets of teachings.

virtue. Positive karma, actions that result in happiness.

white and black actions. Virtuous and nonvirtuous actions respectively. See also *karma*.

white distribution. See *chöd*.

White Umbrella Deity. A female deity practiced to heal sickness, dispel spirit harms and bring auspiciousness.

wish-granting jewel. A jewel that brings its possessor everything that's wished for.

worldly concern. See *eight worldly dharmas*.

Yamantaka. A male meditational deity from the father tantra class of Highest Yoga Tantra.

Yeshe, Lama Thubten (1935–84). Born and educated in Tibet, in 1959 he fled to India, where he met his chief disciple, Lama Zopa Rinpoche. They began teaching Westerners at Kopan Monastery in 1969 and founded the Foundation for the Preservation of the Mahayana Tradition (FPMT) in 1975.

Bibliography

To view or listen to the original teachings from Light of the Path and to follow the online study program connected with these teachings, please see FPMT's Online Learning Center at onlinelearning.fpmt.org.

Chandrakirti. *Introduction to the Middle Way: Chandrakirti's Madhyamakavatara with Commentary by Jamgön Mipham.* Translated by the Padmakara Translation Group. Boston: Shambhala Publications, 2002.

Dagyab Rinpoche. *Buddhist Symbols in Tibetan Culture.* Boston: Wisdom Publications, 1995.

FPMT. *Essential Buddhist Prayers, Volume 1.* Portland: FPMT, 2007.

———. *FPMT Retreat Prayer Book.* Portland: FPMT, 2009.

Govina, Lama Anagarika. *The Way of the White Clouds: A Buddhist Pilgrim in Tibet.* London: Hutchinson, 1968.

Hopkins, Jeffrey. *Tsongkhapa's Final Exposition of Wisdom.* Ithaca: Snow Lion Publications, 2008.

Jinpa, Thupten (translator). *Mind Training: The Great Collection.* Boston: Wisdom Publications, 2006.

Khunu Rinpoche. *Vast as the Heavens, Deep as the Sea: Verses in Praise of Bodhicitta.* Translated by Gareth Sparham. Boston: Wisdom Publications, 1999.

Nagarjuna. *Buddhist Advice for Living and Liberation: Nagarjuna's Precious Garland.* Translated by Jeffrey Hopkins. Ithaca: Snow Lion Publications, 1998.

———. *Nagarjuna's Letter.* Translated by Geshe Lobsang Tharchin and Artemus Engle. Dharamsala: Library of Tibetan Works and Archives, 1995.

Pabongka Rinpoche. *Liberation in Our Hands. Part One: The Preliminaries.* Translated by Sermey Khensur Lobsang Tharchin with Artemus B. Engle. Howell, New Jersey: Mahayana Sutra and Tantra Press, 1990, 2001.

———. *Liberation in Our Hands. Part Two: The Fundamentals.* Translated by Sermey Khensur Lobsang Tharchin with Artemus B. Engle. Howell, New Jersey: Mahayana Sutra and Tantra Press, 1994.

———. *Liberation in Our Hands. Part Three: The Ultimate Goals.* Translated by Sermey Khensur Lobsang Tharchin with Artemus B. Engle. Howell, New Jersey: Mahayana Sutra and Tantra Press, 2001.

———. *Liberation in the Palm of Your Hand.* Edited in the Tibetan by Trijang Rinpoche. Translated by Michael Richards. Boston: Wisdom Publications, 2006.

Shantideva. *A Guide to the Bodhisattva's Way of Life.* Translated by Stephen Batchelor. Dharamsala: Library of Tibetan Works and Archives, 1979, 2007.

———. *A Guide to the Bodhisattva Way of Life.* Translated by Vesna A. Wallace and B. Alan Wallace. Ithaca: Snow Lion Publications, 1997.

Sopa, Geshe Lhundrup. *Steps on the Path to Enlightenment, Volumes 1, 2 & 3.* Boston: Wisdom Publications, 2004, 2005 & 2008.

Tsongkhapa, Lama. *The Great Treatise on the Stages of the Path to Enlightenment, Volume One.* Translated by the Lamrim Chenmo Translation Committee: Ithaca: Snow Lion Publications, 2000.

Thresher, Sarah. *Compassion Training.* Unpublished manuscript. Soquel: Land of Medicine Buddha, 2002.

Zopa Rinpoche, Lama. *The Direct and Unmistaken Method of Purifying and Protecting Yourself.* Portland: FPMT, 2009.

———. *The Door to Satisfaction.* Edited by Ailsa Cameron and Robina Courtin. Boston: Wisdom Publications, 2001.

———. *How to Practice Dharma: Teachings on the Eight Worldly Dharmas.* Edited by Gordon McDougall. Boston: Lama Yeshe Wisdom Archive, 2012.

———. *Practicing the Five Powers near the Time of Death.* Portland: FPMT, 2005.

———. *Service as a Path to Enlightenment.* Portland: FPMT, 2011.

———. *Taking the Essence All Day and Night.* Portland: FPMT, 2010.

———. *Teachings from the Medicine Buddha Retreat.* Edited by Ailsa Cameron. Boston: Lama Yeshe Wisdom Archive, 2009.

———. *Teachings from the Vajrasattva Retreat.* Edited by Ailsa Cameron and Nicholas Ribush. Boston: Lama Yeshe Wisdom Archive, 2000.

——— and Pabongka Rinpoche. *Heart Advice for Retreat.* Portland: FPMT, 2011 (online edition).

Wangmo, Jamyang. *The Lawudo Lama: Stories of Reincarnation from the Mount Everest Region.* Boston: Wisdom Publications, 2005.

Suggested Further Reading

Jinpa, Thupten (translator). *The Book of Kadam*. Boston: Wisdom Publications, 2008.

Zopa Rinpoche, Lama. *The Heart of the Path. Seeing the Guru as Buddha*. Edited by Ailsa Cameron. Boston: Lama Yeshe Wisdom Archive, 2009.

———. *Kadampa Teachings*. Edited by Ailsa Cameron. Boston: Lama Yeshe Wisdom Archive, 2010.

———. *Transforming Problems into Happiness*. Edited by Ailsa Cameron and Robina Courtin. Boston: Wisdom Publications, 2001.

———. *Ultimate Healing*. Edited by Ailsa Cameron. Boston: Wisdom Publications, 2001.

Previously published
by the Lama Yeshe Wisdom Archive

Becoming Your Own Therapist, by Lama Yeshe
Advice for Monks and Nuns, by Lama Yeshe and Lama Zopa Rinpoche
Virtue and Reality, by Lama Zopa Rinpoche
Make Your Mind an Ocean, by Lama Yeshe
Teachings from the Vajrasattva Retreat, by Lama Zopa Rinpoche
The Essence of Tibetan Buddhism, by Lama Yeshe
Daily Purification: A Short Vajrasattva Practice, by Lama Zopa Rinpoche
Making Life Meaningful, by Lama Zopa Rinpoche
Teachings from the Mani Retreat, by Lama Zopa Rinpoche
The Direct and Unmistaken Method, by Lama Zopa Rinpoche
The Yoga of Offering Food, by Lama Zopa Rinpoche
The Peaceful Stillness of the Silent Mind, by Lama Yeshe
Teachings from Tibet, by various great lamas
The Joy of Compassion, by Lama Zopa Rinpoche
The Kindness of Others, by Geshe Jampa Tegchok
Ego, Attachment and Liberation, by Lama Yeshe
How Things Exist, by Lama Zopa Rinpoche
Universal Love, by Lama Yeshe
The Heart of the Path, by Lama Zopa Rinpoche
Teachings from the Medicine Buddha Retreat, by Lama Zopa Rinpoche
Freedom Through Understanding, by Lama Yeshe and Lama Zopa Rinpoche
Kadampa Teachings, by Lama Zopa Rinpoche
Life, Death and After Death, by Lama Yeshe
How to Practice Dharma, by Lama Zopa Rinpoche

For initiates only:

A Teaching on Heruka, by Lama Zopa Rinpoche
A Teaching on Yamantaka, by Lama Zopa Rinpoche

In association with TDL Publications, Los Angeles:

Mirror of Wisdom, by Geshe Tsultim Gyeltsen
Illuminating the Path to Enlightenment, by His Holiness the Dalai Lama

LAMA YESHE WISDOM ARCHIVE

The LAMA YESHE WISDOM ARCHIVE (LYWA) is the collected works of Lama Thubten Yeshe and Lama Thubten Zopa Rinpoche. Lama Zopa Rinpoche, its spiritual director, founded the ARCHIVE in 1996. Lama Yeshe and Lama Zopa Rinpoche began teaching at Kopan Monastery, Nepal, in 1970. Since then, their teachings have been recorded and transcribed. At present we have well over 10,000 hours of digital audio and some 70,000 pages of raw transcript. Many recordings, mostly teachings by Lama Zopa Rinpoche, remain to be transcribed, and as Rinpoche continues to teach, the number of recordings in the ARCHIVE increases accordingly. Most of our transcripts have been neither checked nor edited.

Here at the LYWA we are making every effort to organize the transcription of that which has not yet been transcribed, edit that which has not yet been edited, and generally do the many other tasks detailed below.

The work of the LAMA YESHE WISDOM ARCHIVE falls into two categories: archiving and dissemination.

Archiving requires managing the recordings of teachings by Lama Yeshe and Lama Zopa Rinpoche that have already been collected, collecting recordings of teachings given but not yet sent to the ARCHIVE, and collecting recordings of Lama Zopa's on-going teachings, talks, advice and so forth as he travels the world for the benefit of all. Incoming media are then catalogued and stored safely while being kept accessible for further work.

We organize the transcription of audio, add the transcripts to the already existent database of teachings, manage this database, have transcripts checked, and make transcripts available to editors or others doing research on or practicing these teachings.

Other archiving activities include working with video and photographs of the Lamas and digitizing ARCHIVE materials.

Dissemination involves making the Lamas' teachings available through various avenues including books for free distribution and sale, lightly edited transcripts, a monthly e-letter (see below), DVDs, articles in *Mandala* and other magazines and on our website. Irrespective of the medium we choose, the teachings require a significant amount of work to prepare them for distribution.

This is just a summary of what we do. The ARCHIVE was established with virtually no seed funding and has developed solely through the kindness of many people, some of whom we have mentioned at the front of this book and most of the others on our website. We sincerely thank them all.

Our further development similarly depends upon the generosity of those who see the benefit and necessity of this work, and we would be extremely grateful for your help. Thus we hereby appeal to you for your kind support. If you would like to make a contribution to help us with any of the above tasks or to sponsor books for free distribution, please contact us:

LAMA YESHE WISDOM ARCHIVE
PO Box 636, Lincoln, MA 01773, USA
Telephone (781) 259-4466
info@LamaYeshe.com
WWW.LAMAYESHE.COM

The LAMA YESHE WISDOM ARCHIVE is a 501(c)(3) tax-deductible, non-profit corporation dedicated to the welfare of all sentient beings and totally dependent upon your donations for its continued existence. Thank you so much for your support. You may contribute by mailing a check, bank draft or money order to our Lincoln address; by making a donation on our secure website; by mailing us your credit card number or phoning it in; or by transferring funds directly to our bank—ask us for details.

LAMA YESHE WISDOM ARCHIVE MEMBERSHIP

In order to raise the money we need to employ editors to make available the thousands of hours of teachings mentioned above, we have established a membership plan. Membership costs US$1,000 and its main benefit is that you will be helping make the Lamas' incredible teachings available to a worldwide audience. More direct and tangible benefits to you personally include free Lama Yeshe and Lama Zopa Rinpoche books from the ARCHIVE and Wisdom Publications, a year's subscription to *Mandala*, a year of monthly pujas by the monks and nuns at Kopan Monastery with your personal dedication, and access to an exclusive members-only section of our website containing the entire LYWA library of publications in electronic format. Please see www.LamaYeshe.com for more information.

MONTHLY E-LETTER

Each month we send out a free e-letter containing our latest news and a previously unpublished teaching by Lama Yeshe or Lama Zopa Rinpoche. To see over one hundred back-issues or to subscribe with your email address, please go to our website.

The Foundation for the Preservation of the Mahayana Tradition

The Foundation for the Preservation of the Mahayana Tradition (FPMT) is an international organization of Buddhist meditation study and retreat centers, both urban and rural, monasteries, publishing houses, healing centers and other related activities founded in 1975 by Lama Thubten Yeshe and Lama Thubten Zopa Rinpoche. At present, there are more than 160 FPMT centers and related activities in over thirty countries worldwide.

The FPMT has been established to facilitate the study and practice of Mahayana Buddhism in general and the Tibetan Gelug tradition, founded in the fifteenth century by the great scholar, yogi and saint, Lama Je Tsongkhapa, in particular.

Every quarter, the Foundation publishes a wonderful news journal, *Mandala*, from its International Office in the United States of America. To subscribe or view back issues, please go to the *Mandala* website, www. mandalamagazine.org, or contact:

FPMT
1632 SE 11th Avenue, Portland, OR 97214
Telephone (503) 808-1588; Fax (503) 808-1589
info@fpmt.org
WWW.FPMT.ORG

The FPMT website also offers teachings by His Holiness the Dalai Lama, Lama Yeshe, Lama Zopa Rinpoche and many other highly respected teachers in the tradition, details about the FPMT's educational programs, audio through FPMT radio, a complete listing of FPMT centers all over the world and in your area, a link to the excellent FPMT Store, and links to FPMT centers on the web, where you will find details of their programs, and to other interesting Buddhist and Tibetan home pages.

FPMT Online Learning Center

In 2009, FPMT Education Services launched the FPMT Online Learning Center to make FPMT education programs and materials more accessible to students worldwide. While continuing to expand, the Online Learning Center currently offers the following courses:

- Meditation 101
- Buddhism in a Nutshell
- Heart Advice for Death and Dying
- Discovering Buddhism
- Basic Program
- Living in the Path

Living in the Path is particularly unique in that it takes teachings by Lama Zopa Rinpoche and presents them in theme-related modules that include teaching transcripts, video extracts, meditations, mindfulness practices, karma yoga, and questions to assist students in integrating the material. If you are inspired to experience the teachings contained in *Bodhisattva Attitude* directly from Rinpoche, please participate in the first two modules of Living in the Path. Current modules include: *Motivation for Life, Taking the Essence, What Buddhists Believe, Guru is Buddha, Introduction to Atisha's text, The Happiness of Dharma, Bringing Emptiness to Life, The Secret of the Mind, Diamond Cutter Meditation,* and *Refuge & Bodhichitta.*

All of our online programs provide audio and/or video teachings of the subjects, guided meditations, readings, and other support materials. Online forums for each program provide students the opportunity to discuss the subject matter and to ask questions of forum elders. Additionally, many retreats led by Lama Zopa Rinpoche are available in full via audio and/or video format.

Education Services is committed to creating a dynamic virtual learning environment and adding more FPMT programming and materials for you to enjoy via the Online Learning Center.

Visit us at: onlinelearning.fpmt.org

Other teachings of Lama Yeshe and Lama Zopa Rinpoche currently available

Books published by Wisdom Publications

Wisdom Energy, by Lama Yeshe and Lama Zopa Rinpoche
Introduction to Tantra, by Lama Yeshe
Transforming Problems, by Lama Zopa Rinpoche
The Door to Satisfaction, by Lama Zopa Rinpoche
Becoming Vajrasattva: The Tantric Path of Purification, by Lama Yeshe
The Bliss of Inner Fire, by Lama Yeshe
Becoming the Compassion Buddha, by Lama Yeshe
Ultimate Healing, by Lama Zopa Rinpoche
Dear Lama Zopa, by Lama Zopa Rinpoche
How to Be Happy, by Lama Zopa Rinpoche
Wholesome Fear, by Lama Zopa Rinpoche with Kathleen McDonald
When the Chocolate Runs Out, by Lama Yeshe

About Lama Yeshe:

Reincarnation: The Boy Lama, by Vicki Mackenzie

About Lama Zopa Rinpoche:

The Lawudo Lama, by Jamyang Wangmo
You can get more information about and order the above titles at www.wisdom-pubs.org or call toll free in the USA on 1-800-272-4050.

Transcripts, practices and other materials

See the LYWA and FPMT websites for transcripts of teachings by Lama Yeshe and Lama Zopa Rinpoche and other practices written or compiled by Lama Zopa Rinpoche.

DVDs of Lama Yeshe

We are in the process of converting our VHS videos of Lama Yeshe's teachings to DVD. *The Three Principal Aspects of the Path, Introduction to Tantra, Offering Tsok to Heruka Vajrasattva, Anxiety in the Nuclear Age, Bringing Dharma to the West, Lama Yeshe at Disneyland, Freedom Through Understanding* and *Life, Death and After Death* are currently available. More coming all the time—see our website for details.

DVDs of Lama Zopa Rinpoche

There are many available: see the Store on the FPMT website for more information.

What to do with Dharma teachings

The Buddhadharma is the true source of happiness for all sentient beings. Books like this show you how to put the teachings into practice and integrate them into your life, whereby you get the happiness you seek. Therefore, anything containing Dharma teachings, the names of your teachers or holy images is more precious than other material objects and should be treated with respect. To avoid creating the karma of not meeting the Dharma again in future lives, please do not put books (or other holy objects) on the floor or underneath other stuff, step over or sit upon them, or use them for mundane purposes such as propping up wobbly tables. They should be kept in a clean, high place, separate from worldly writings, and wrapped in cloth when being carried around. These are but a few considerations.

Should you need to get rid of Dharma materials, they should not be thrown in the rubbish but burned in a special way. Briefly: do not incinerate such materials with other trash, but alone, and as they burn, recite the mantra OM AH HUM. As the smoke rises, visualize that it pervades all of space, carrying the essence of the Dharma to all sentient beings in the six samsaric realms, purifying their minds, alleviating their suffering, and bringing them all happiness, up to and including enlightenment. Some people might find this practice a bit unusual, but it is given according to tradition. Thank you very much.

Dedication

Through the merit created by preparing, reading, thinking about and sharing this book with others, may all teachers of the Dharma live long and healthy lives, may the Dharma spread throughout the infinite reaches of space, and may all sentient beings quickly attain enlightenment.

In whichever realm, country, area or place this book may be, may there be no war, drought, famine, disease, injury, disharmony or unhappiness, may there be only great prosperity, may everything needed be easily obtained, and may all be guided by only perfectly qualified Dharma teachers, enjoy the happiness of Dharma, have love and compassion for all sentient beings, and only benefit and never harm each other.

LAMA THUBTEN ZOPA RINPOCHE was born in Thangme, Nepal, in 1945. At the age of three he was recognized as the reincarnation of the Lawudo Lama, who had lived nearby at Lawudo, within sight of Rinpoche's Thangme home. Rinpoche's own description of his early years may be found in his book, *The Door to Satisfaction*. At the age of ten, Rinpoche went to Tibet and studied and meditated at Domo Geshe Rinpoche's monastery near Pagri, until the Chinese occupation of Tibet in 1959 forced him to forsake Tibet for the safety of Bhutan. Rinpoche then went to the Tibetan refugee camp at Buxa Duar, West Bengal, India, where he met Lama Yeshe, who became his closest teacher. The Lamas went to Nepal in 1967, and over the next few years built Kopan and Lawudo Monasteries. In 1971 Lama Zopa Rinpoche gave the first of his famous annual lam-rim retreat courses, which continue at Kopan to this day. In 1974, with Lama Yeshe, Rinpoche began traveling the world to teach and establish centers of Dharma. When Lama Yeshe passed away in 1984, Rinpoche took over as spiritual head of the FPMT, which has continued to flourish under his peerless leadership. More details of Rinpoche's life and work may be found in *The Lawudo Lama* and on the LYWA and FPMT websites. In addition to many LYWA and FPMT books, Rinpoche's other published teachings include *Wisdom Energy* (with Lama Yeshe), *Transforming Problems, Ultimate Healing, Dear Lama Zopa, How to Be Happy, Wholesome Fear* and many transcripts and practice booklets.

SARAH THRESHER graduated with a BA Honors degree in English in 1982 and shortly afterwards met Lama Zopa Rinpoche and Lama Yeshe at her first Buddhist course in Kopan Monastery, Nepal. In 1983 she began work as an editor for Wisdom Publications and over the next nine years was involved in several major publishing projects, including Pabongka Rinpoche's *Liberation in the Palm of Your Hand* and His Holiness Dudjom Rinpoche's *History and Fundamentals of the Nyingma School*. She ordained in 1986 and began teaching full time in 1992. Since that time, she has travelled and taught in countries around the world. Over the past ten years she has assisted Lama Zopa Rinpoche in leading several major retreats under his guidance and is particularly interested in preserving Rinpoche's style and way of doing things. She is currently an FPMT Touring Teacher based in the USA and editor of LYWA's Heart Advice Series.